SOLO GOLF

The Zen of Playing Alone and How It Can Transform Your Game

GARY BELSKY

WORKMAN PUBLISHING • NEW YORK

Workman
Workman Publishing
Hachette Book Group, Inc.
1290 Avenue of the Americas
New York, NY 10104
workman.com

Workman is an imprint of Workman Publishing, a division of Hachette Book Group, Inc. The Workman name and logo are registered trademarks of Hachette Book Group, Inc.

Design by Jack Dennington

Additional photo credits information is on page 150.

Library of Congress Cataloging-in-Publication Data is on file.

ISBNs 978-1-5235-2942-1 (paperback), 978-1-5235-2944-5 (ebook)

First Edition March 2026

Printed in China (1010) on responsibly sourced paper

10 9 8 7 6 5 4 3 2 1

To David, Ari, Mo, Adir, Jay Z, Russ, Mark, and Barry—my preferred course companions over the years (except when I preferred none).

CONTENTS

PART III

The Practical

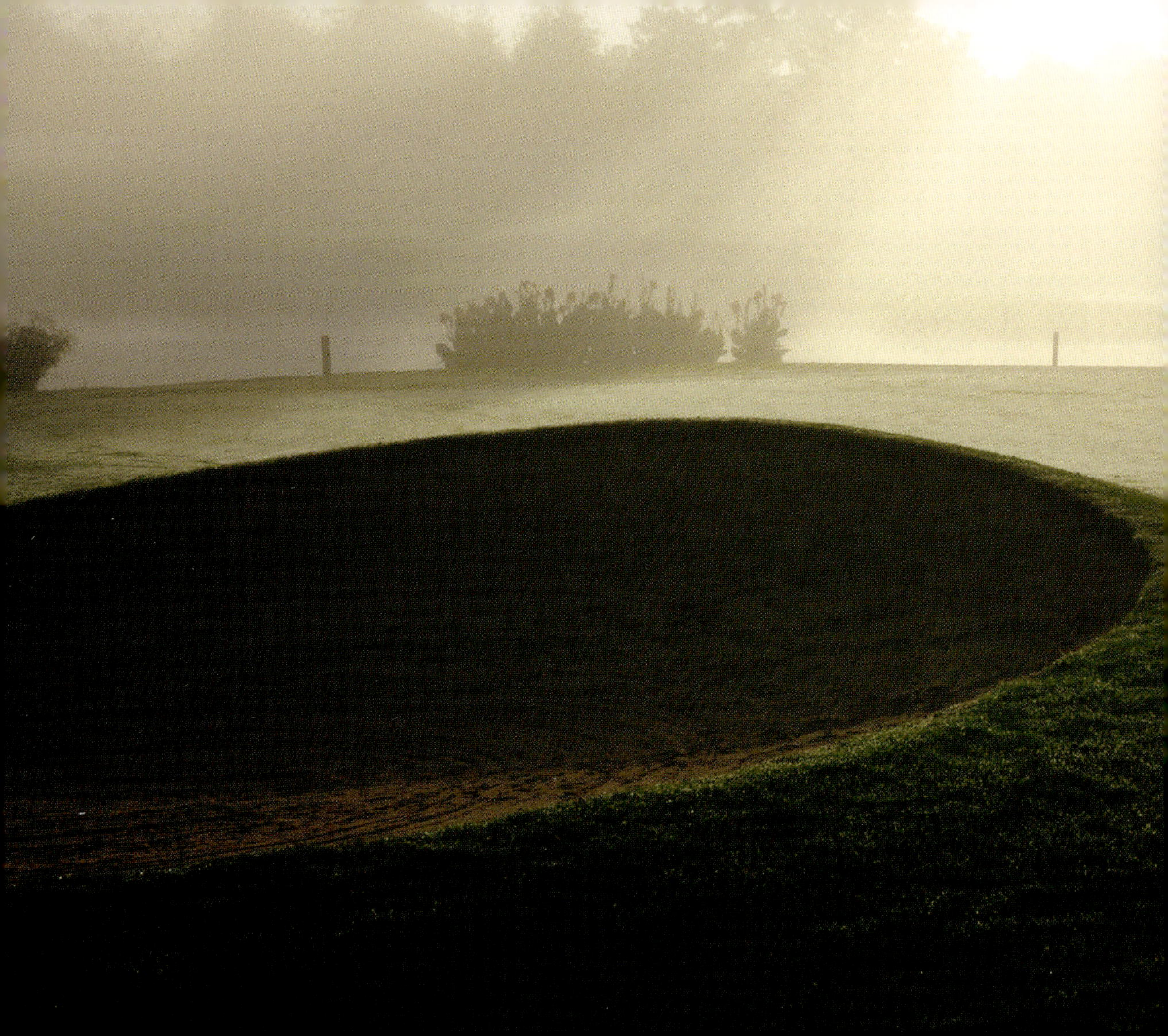

solo golf

sō-(ˌ)lō gälf ***noun:***

(1) a game in which one person, unaccompanied by any other person, plays a game most people consider a group activity; **(2)** a onesome; **(3)** the subject of a little book.

•

Example of solo golf *in a sentence:* Playing solo golf this morning, I realized again how much fun I have when it's just me, my clubs, and an open course.

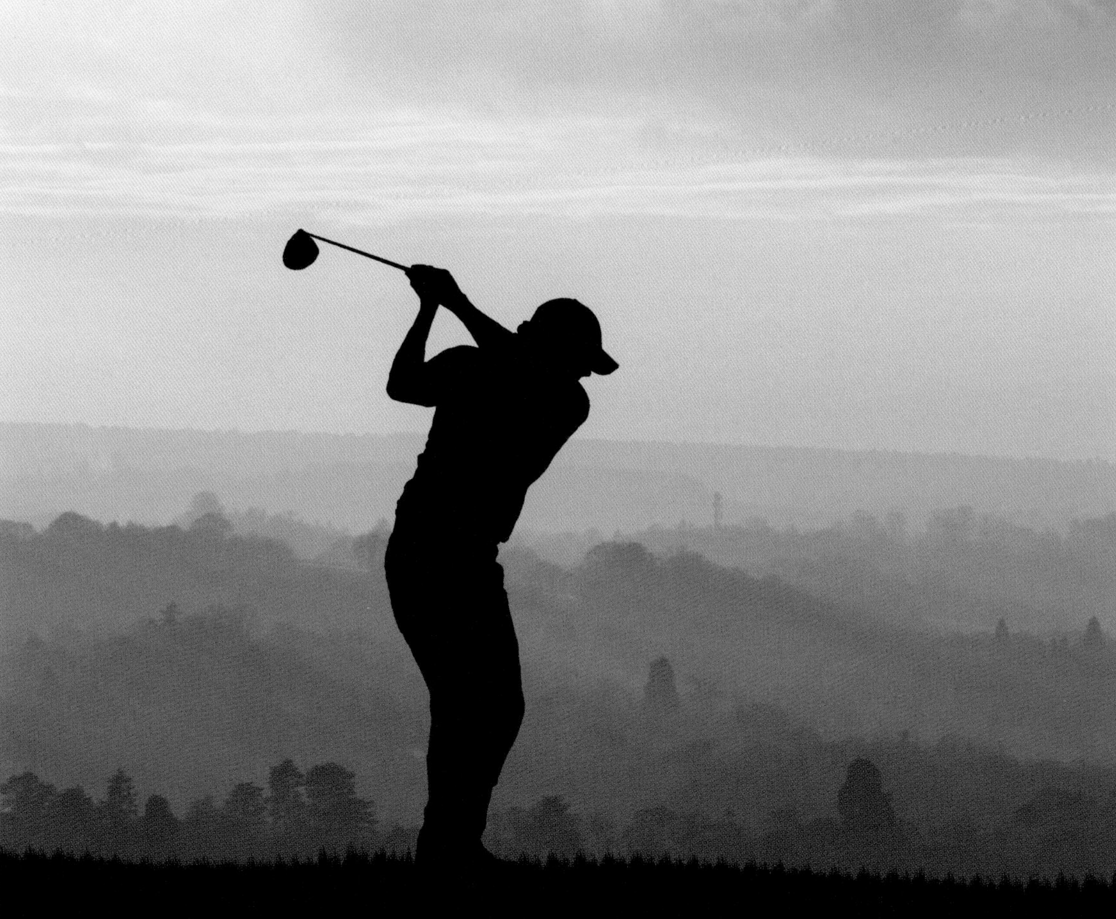

INTRODUCTION

How It All Began

It must be said at the outset of this book that the game of golf was created by loners. Long before golf was a clubby pastime for sociable types, it was something much closer to a distraction—a self-invented game to stave off boredom on the windblown, barely arable coastlines of eastern Scotland. These stretches of land, beautiful but agriculturally useless, were left mostly to the sea, the sheep, and their shepherds. And those shepherds, often alone for hours or days, did what many people do when no one's watching: They made something up.

In this case, that "something" was a game built out of what they had—sticks, stones, tufts of grass, and a lot of time. They took aim at natural landmarks or whatever holes the local burrowing creatures had kindly left behind, treating the terrain less like a workplace and more like a lightly curated playground. The rules weren't written, the equipment wasn't standardized, and no one had yet coined the term *tee time*. But the bones of the game were there, and it was solitary, improvised, and quietly obsessive. Meanwhile, loners in other parts of the world developed similar time-wasting habits—which is why some people in the Netherlands, China, and elsewhere stake a claim to golf's invention.

I bring this up now to get ahead of a common concern about the topic of this book: that playing solo golf—i.e., by yourself, without other golfers—robs the game of its natural sociability.

To be clear, I enjoy a golf foursome with friends, relatives, and even strangers as much as the next duffer. I am the farthest thing from an introvert that you can imagine, and there is nothing about my game that causes me shame or demands that it be played in private. I am plausibly capable of shooting par on most holes, and when par is not plausible, I know to pick up my ball if and when my game has gone sideways.

No, the solo rounds I sometimes choose to play are nothing more or less than a joyful, meditative, and lesson-filled *accent* to my core golf activities, which usually involve nephews or close friends. I love few things more than taking a long, lazy, and crooked walk in nature with people I like, stopping every so often to swing with purpose at a little, white, dimpled ball.

I like playing golf with other humans so much, in fact, that this book might never have come about were it not for a business trip I took many years ago to Seattle. Before leaving on that long-ago journey, I knew I would have a day free between meetings, so I brought my clubs with me, hoping to find time for a round on an unfamiliar track.

A couple of days later, when I called the Gleneagle Golf Course north of Seattle, which had only just recently opened, the guy who answered the phone in the pro shop told me to come by whenever I liked. But when I arrived late the next morning, the course blanketed in a light mist, there was no other golfer in sight. "If you want to play right now," the pro shop guy told me, "I'll have to send you out on your own."

I paused before answering, and not just because I had never played by myself. Conflicting thoughts sliced incompatibly through my head, ranging from *Who will help me find my ball if I manage to keep my head down?* to *Who's going to sign my scorecard when I notch my first hole in one?*

Nevertheless, low expectations and high hopes aside, I didn't want to risk the weather worsening as I waited for a partner, so I decided to go it alone. I also opted to walk the course, forgoing even a handcart on the silver-lining presumption that at the very least I would get a good workout from carrying my bag for a few miles.

What I got, as it turned out, was far more beneficial than strength training or light cardio. What I got was sporting transcendence. Although I do not remember playing especially well or poorly, I recall with absolute clarity the frame of mind I achieved during those few hours. It was like nothing I had ever experienced.

It was something that I frequently describe as "Zen golf": peaceful, meditative, intuitive, unearthly.

Alone and undistracted in a Garden of Eden of greens and browns, I marveled at the lush beauty of nature, selectively manicured.

Alone and unwatched by people with or behind me, I swung my clubs with an unselfconscious ease that I had never before experienced on a golf course.

Alone and unbothered by competition, I chose every club in a carefree spirit of experimentation and curiosity.

Alone and unaffected by the pressures of friendly bets, I reviewed every flushed iron and skulled chip with the same unself-critical desire to understand what went right and what did not.

Alone and undistracted by playing partner chitchat, I *heard* golf in a way I never had—the soft cracking of spikes on cart paths, the rat-a-tat-tat of raindrops on leaves, the blissful echo of a long putt rattling around the bottom of a cup.

Alone and undisturbed by pretty much anything, I unintentionally distilled golf to its essence: one person, one set of clubs, and a joyful urge to propel a ball down fairways, around trees, over water, out of sand, and into holes.

Golf, in other words, that's not too far from the game that some lonely shepherds long ago imagined into existence. It's a game that I hope to persuade you to try as part of your golf outing repertoire, while also providing useful advice on how to go about it.

With all of the above in mind, I've organized this book into three sections:

THE MYSTICAL

Concerning the otherworldly experience of playing solo golf

THE EXPERIMENTAL

Regarding the many variations and benefits of playing by yourself

THE PRACTICAL

Advice on securing time alone in a sport that is geared toward group fun

Here's hoping that you get as much from reading about solo golf as I get from playing it.

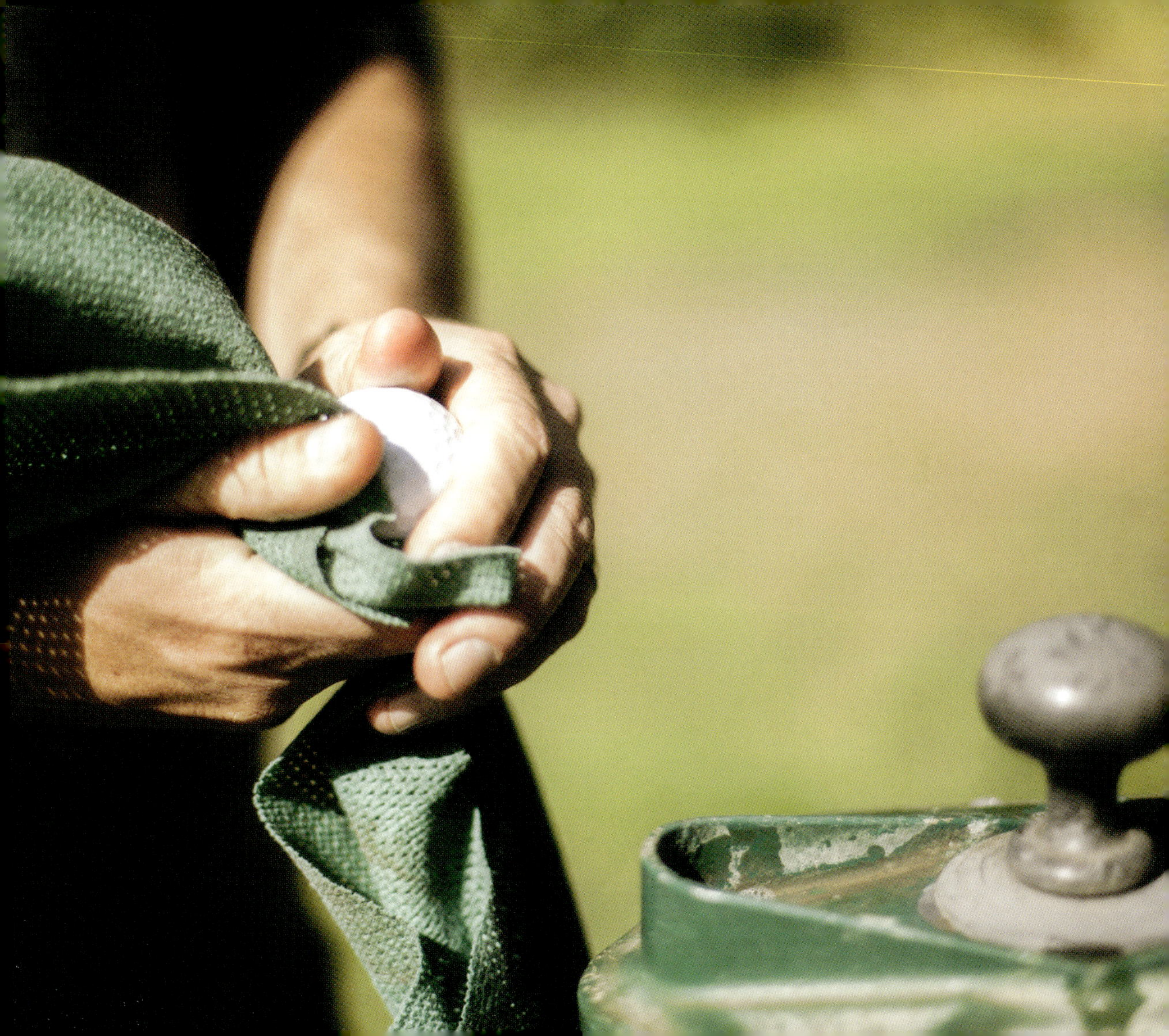

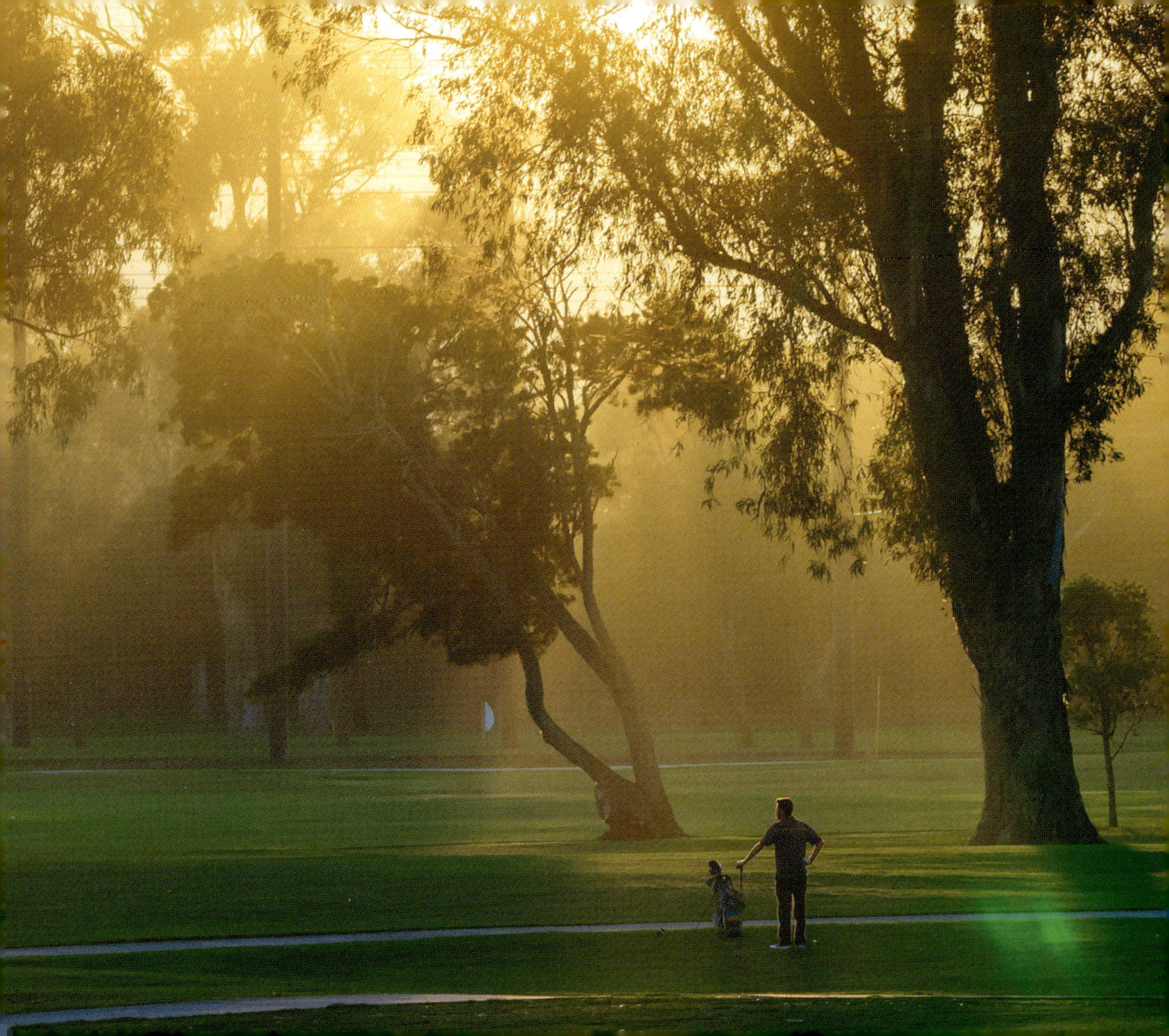

PART I

THE MYSTICAL

Before you explain it, before you optimize it, you have to feel it. This section explores the emotional and psychological draw of playing golf alone—the serenity it brings, the clarity it invites, the many and varied ways it softens time and sharpens intention. And, no, you don't have to be spiritually minded to find something sacred in the solo golf experience. You just have to be open to a new way of playing the game.

"Golf is the only sport that offers enough solitude and silence for the soul to play a decisive part."

—BOBBY JONES, *first Grand Slam winner*

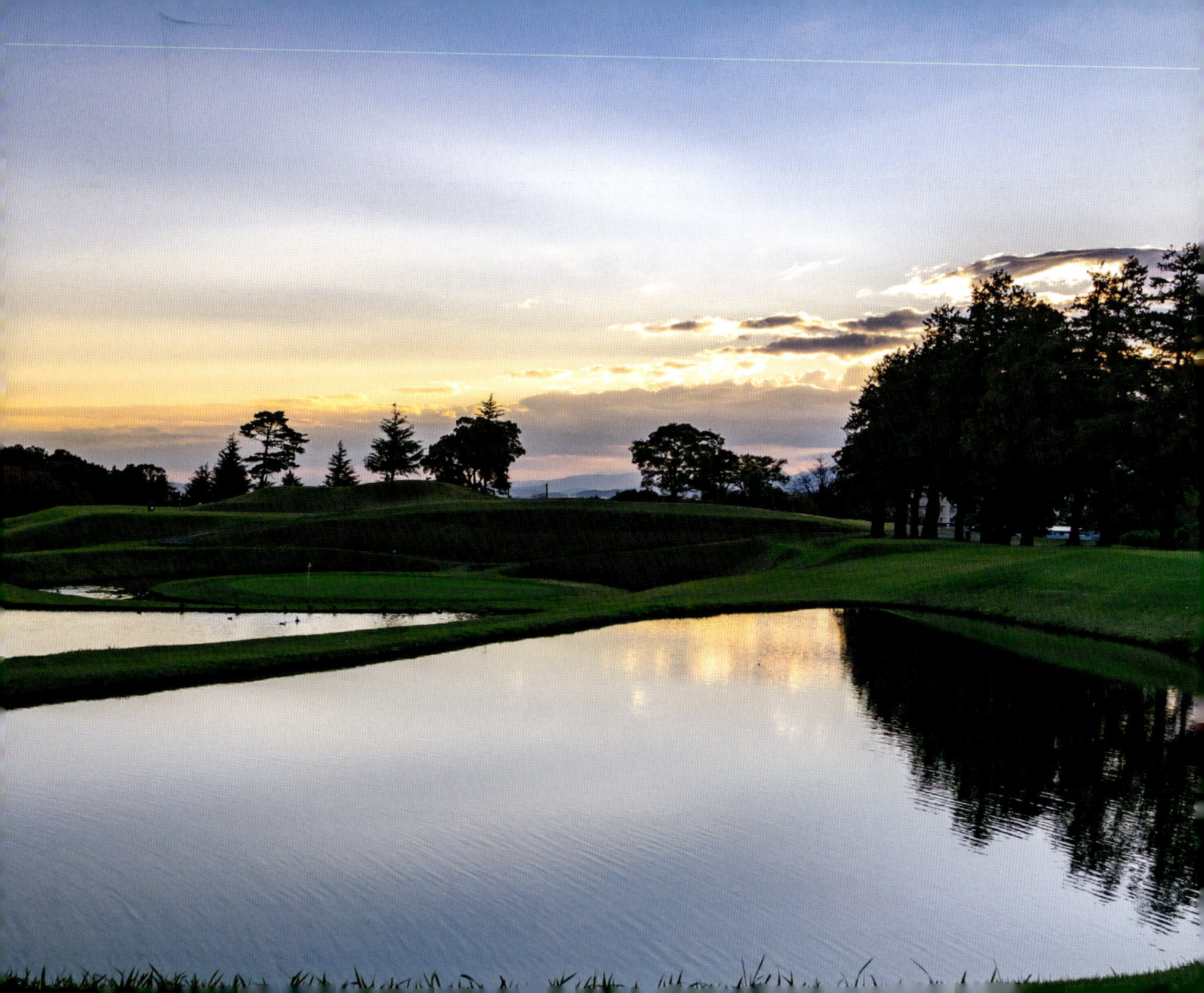

A Meditation on Solitude

There may be no lonelier place in the world than an empty golf course. Golf, after all, is both a sport and a pastime that typically pulses with commotion, from the banter and clatter of the people in one's own playing group, to the low-hum activity of other folks within ear- and eyeshot on most courses, to the crowded galleries, production setups, and course officials—not to mention golfers and caddies—of televised tournaments.

But when people first have a go at solo golf, the newfound feeling of solitude is often the most jarring aspect. It is an experience that generally happens in the wee or fading hours of golf course operation, hours in the day when most of the other humans are few and far between.

At first, this emptiness can feel almost eerie, like walking into an abandoned theater or school building long after the final bell. The absence of voices, footsteps, and general commotion creates a vacuum, one that amplifies every other sound—the rustle of grass, the crack of club striking ball, even your own breathing. The vast quiet is not just around you; it seems to seep into you as well, penetrating your bones and your thoughts.

But if the isolation, seclusion, and privacy of solo golf can take some getting used to, those qualities quickly rank high among the main attractions, even for the most extroverted among us. That's doubtless because, in a world of increasingly loud and seemingly unavoidable distractions, there are few people who don't appreciate genuine opportunities for "alone time."

In fact, it's not just a luxury; it's a necessity. Psychologists—both practitioners and researchers—regularly emphasize the importance of periodic solitude for mental health, describing it as an unparalleled opportunity for the mind to recalibrate and process the world without interference. Solo golf offers this in abundance: time and space where the only conversation is the one happening inside your own head.

But the benefits accrue even faster when withdrawals from social interaction involve a genuine immersion in nature, the sort of calming sensory experience that a growing body of research has shown to be physically relaxing and spiritually nourishing. The Japanese have a phrase—*shinrin-yoku*, or "forest bathing"—to describe the simple act of spending unhurried time in the woods, taking in the air, the light, the smells, the quiet. No goals, no gear, no phones. Just you and the forest, and whatever happens when you let your senses do the work. It's an old practice with a growing following, mostly because it turns out that being around trees is good for you—body, mind, and otherwise.

On a golf course, this immersion is heightened by the very act of walking. Moving from tee to green becomes a kind of pilgrimage, with each step drawing you deeper into the environment. The rhythm of your pace syncs with the rhythm of the game, creating a sense of unity between player and place.

And, of course, for all the precise landscaping of most golf courses, there's something primordial in the feeling one has when standing alone in nature: strolling through fescue or zoysia, maybe a light breeze to rustle the trees or trouble the otherwise placid lake that guards the green. It's a wonder any time, but all the more so during "me time."

Combine such quiet and peacefulness with familiar, repetitive action—like, say, a pre-shot routine or (ideally) a golf swing—and one can very quickly enter into a "flow state."

"Flow," as some readers know, is a state of mind in which a person is so focused on a specific task or activity that they experience few if any thoughts about themselves or their performance. The "thing" they are doing—be it sweater knitting, backyard gardening, software coding, or playing golf—becomes all-consuming in the most positive understanding of that term.

This flow, not for nothing, isn't about perfection or performance; rather, it's about presence. In these moments, your swing feels effortless, the ball seems to obey without resistance, and time itself can stretch or contract. It's not a matter of trying harder but rather of disappearing into the act.

And taken together, the components that make up the solo golf experience—solitude, nature, flow—can feel like a gift from the golf gods.

Given only to you.

YOU HAVE TO LAUGH

There are, in any objective accounting, an infinite number of golf jokes. But there is one, by any subjective measure, that's the most revealing about most golfers:

Joe was having a tough day—24 over par through 17, with too many lost balls to count—when his caddie coughed during his backswing on the final tee.

"You might be the worst caddie in the world!" Joe yelled after slicing his ball into the woods.

"I doubt it," his caddie replied. "That would be too much of a coincidence."

To be clear, there's nothing particularly funny about lost golf balls. But this old chestnut addresses a major drawback to solo golf: When you play golf alone, there's no one to track the flight of your ball. There's also no one to show you the line for a putt or help you calculate distances; I cannot and will not sugarcoat it. Balls cost money in addition to strokes.

So, before I send you to a local track all by your lonesome, I am obliged to leave you with three related thoughts about golf balls:

1. Solo golf is what used balls are meant for.
2. Ditto for neon-colored balls.
3. You will lose more balls playing solo than you do playing with others.

The sooner a solo golfer accepts No. 3, the more enjoyable their experience will be. Or, to paraphrase the great American novelist Willa Cather, "The golf is all; the ball is nothing."

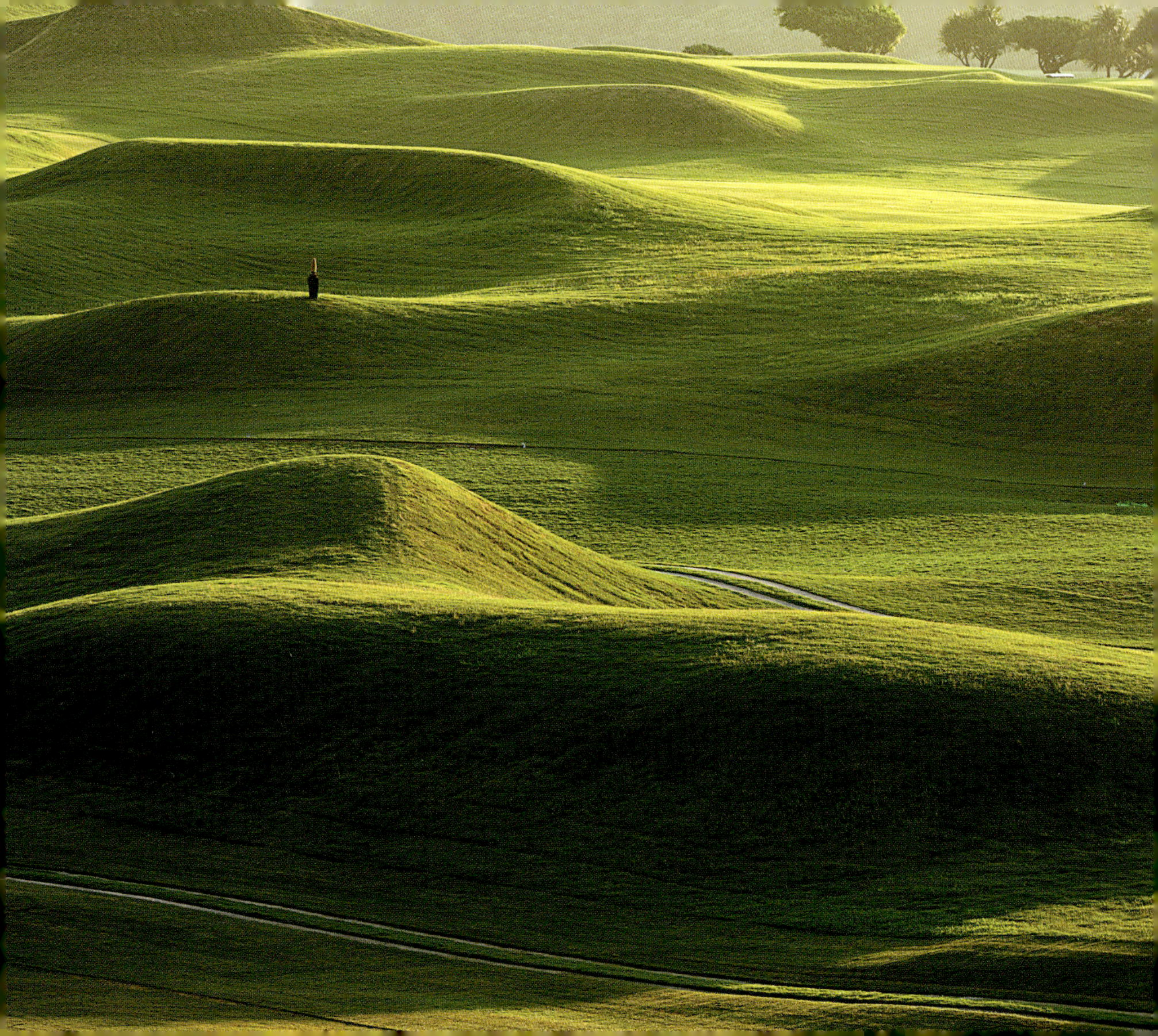

"For this game you need, above all things, to be in a tranquil frame of mind."

—HARRY VARDON,

six-time British Open champion

A Meditation on Sound

Every golfer can immediately conjure the aural experience: a soft plop, round and hollow, just a scratch note of grit, amplified by the faintest of echoes.

It is the sound of a golf ball falling into the cup, and if the description calls to mind a wine connoisseur describing a favorite Barolo, well, that is what solo golf will do to even the least sentimental or pretentious practitioner. Think of it as golf ASMR (i.e., that transfixing, tingling sensation you get from certain sounds like whispering, crinkling, or Tiger Woods flushing irons at the Masters).

Golf is not especially known for its acoustics. People can easily conjure (and recognize) the crack of a baseball hitting the sweet spot of a bat, the crash of 10 bowling pins in a well-thrown strike, the swish of a nothing-but-net shot in basketball, or the roar of a perfectly tuned stock-car engine, but you'd be hard pressed to find familiar language for most of the components of a golf game (see a brief guide on pages 20–21). You'd be even harder pressed to find yourself in a conversation about golf noises while sitting at the bar in your local 19th hole.

But if most golfers generally don't discuss the sounds of the game during group play, the aural aspects are a central part of the solo experience.

In the average round of golf there's of course an awful lot of chatter, both specific to the sport (e.g., "Nice shot," "You're away," "Head down," "What's wrong with me?!") and general to the species (e.g., "How's the family?" "What line of work are you in?" "Next round's on me"). Although etiquette and common courtesy call for silence when someone is preparing to take a shot or is in the middle of one, there's rarely a moment otherwise when someone isn't talking somewhere nearby.

So, when you play solo golf, you will quickly find yourself noticing and savoring a round's numerous and varied noises, most of them soothing and many of them easily missed when in the company of other golfers.

Alone on a course, though—and especially in the quiet of an early morning, late afternoon, or remote setting—you will be able to appraise your efforts and predict their results with uncanny accuracy, based solely on the sounds those efforts produce. From a crushed drive to a sweet wedge, you will *hear* the strength in your game as much as you see or feel it. Alas, the same is true for when skill abandons you, whether from a dissonant topping or the crack of a ball hitting a tree, out of sight (and out of bounds).

And the beauty of solo golf is that the soundscape is not limited to just the mechanics of the game itself. Without the hum of conversation or the *clakket*ting of clubs being jostled in a group setting, your ears tune in to details that might otherwise go unnoticed. The rhythmic chirp of crickets or wafts of birdsong, the low rustle of leaves stirred by the breeze, the satisfying snap of a twig underfoot as you walk between shots—all of these sounds layer together to create an experience that is as meditative as it is immersive.

Even the mundane noises of a round—the bristled friction of ball-washer brush on ball, the crisp tear of Velcro as you adjust your glove—take on a richness when amplified by solitude.

Sometimes, even on your worst of days, you will find enormous comfort and calm in the gentle scratch of cleats on a cart path or the dull thud of a sky-high approach shot dropping safely onto the green—whether it's your second shot or your fifth.

And sometimes, the worst of holes can be redeemed by the sweetest of sounds. The *plop* of a perfect chip into the cup. The *whiz* of a drive that just feels right. The soft crunch of grass underfoot as you retrieve your ball.

When playing solo, the sounds of golf aren't just part of the game. They *are* the game.

In a solo round, golf's beauty is not only seen but heard.

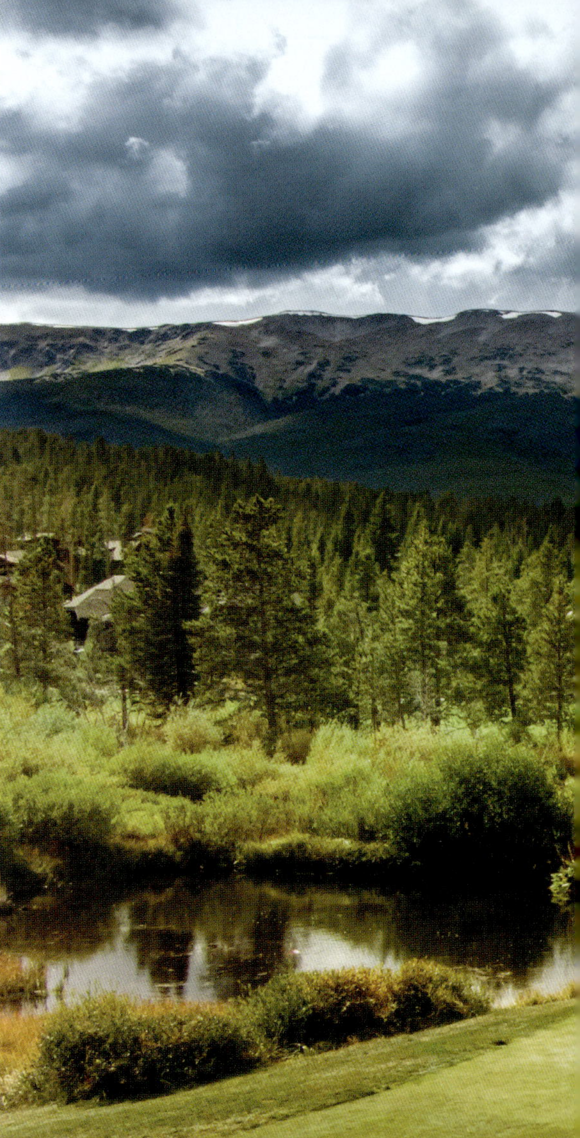

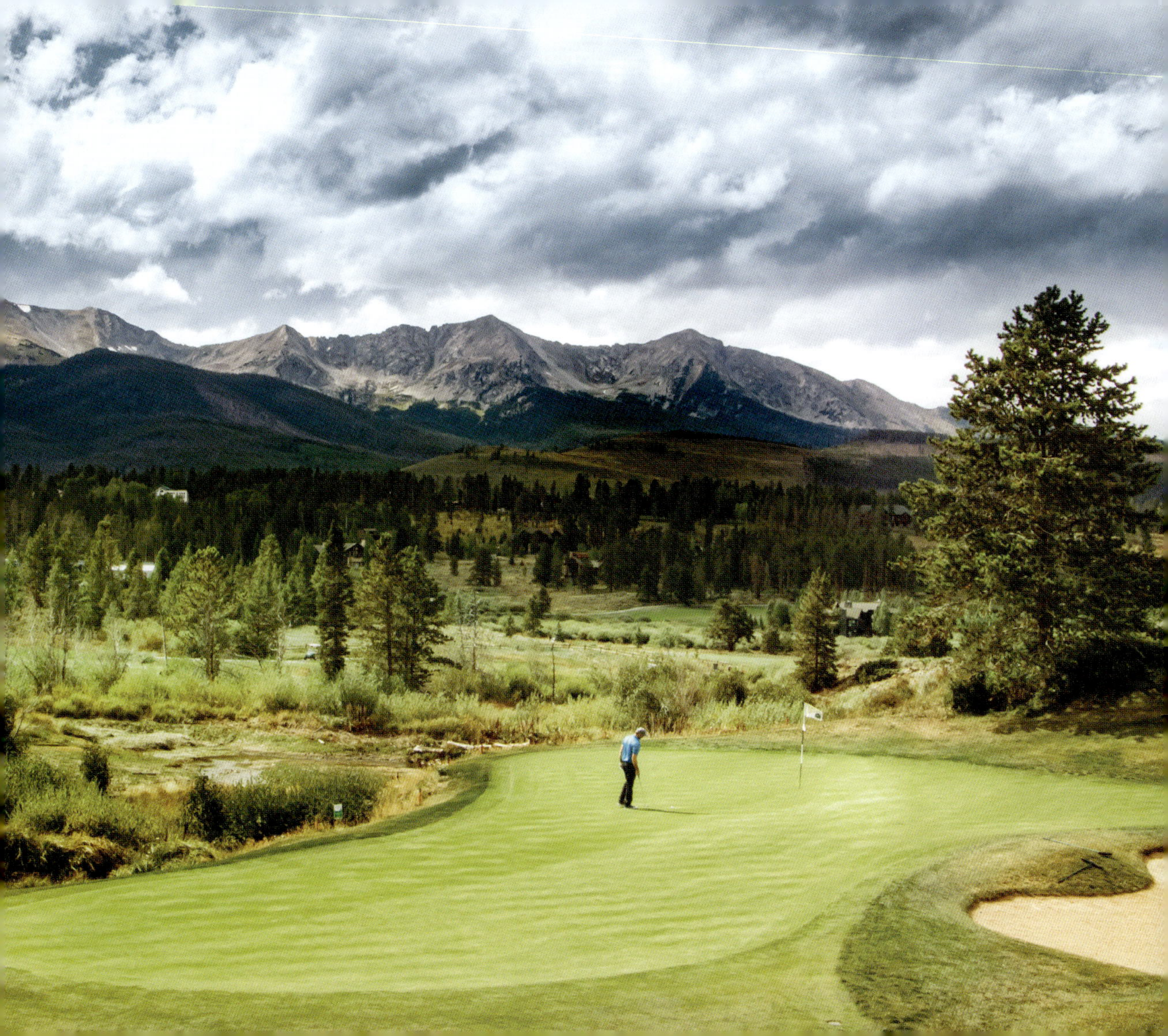

TOP 15 GOLF SOUNDS: AN ONOMATOPOEIC GUIDE

1. ***PLAHHHP.***
   Ball falling into the cup. That sweet, hollow punctuation mark that says, "This hole is done." No matter how many strokes it took, this sound always feels like closure, as if a door has closed behind you.

2. ***THWACK.***
   Perfectly squared driver hitting the ball. The ultimate affirmation of a job well done, it is the sound you dream of when you wake up for an early tee time: crisp, sharp, and reverberating with potential as your ball soars into the fairway.

3. ***THWACK-KEENK.***
   Perfectly squared driver hitting the ball that also catches the top of the tee. This is also known as the bonus sound of absolute perfection, performed with flair, and of doing everything right.

4. ***PPHLUNK.***
   Ball landing on the green from a significant height. It's the sound of a mini celebration as your ball lands pointedly where you wanted it to. Bonus points for the faint backspin *fffft* if it really stops dead.

5. ***THUMP.***
   Wedge slapping sand in the trap. Deep and satisfying, this sound is gritty determination made audible, whether or not the ball listens.

6. ***FLISHT.***
   Blade sweeping grass on a practice swing. A whisper of possibility. It's the preview of greatness—if only the real swing can match it. Often accompanied by an internal monologue: *Now just do that again.*

7. ***THHHHTT.***
   Ball barely grazing a branch. A soft hiss that carries big consequences. It's subtle enough that you might not notice it right away—until you see where your ball lands.

8. ***CLACKETT.***
Clubs rattling when a golf bag is lifted. The sound of adventure beginning. Whether you're heading to the first tee or walking to the car after a satisfying round, this cheerful jangle says, "Here we go."

9. ***SCRAHNTK.***
Cleats on concrete. The official soundtrack of golf transition. It's the sound of intent, of moving with purpose toward the next challenge—or the clubhouse.

10. ***SSHHWIP.***
Roped drive cutting through the wind. This hum of pure energy, like a slingshot in action, is the sound of a ball doing exactly what it's supposed to: cutting the air with purpose and speed.

11. ***PHAAP.***
Putter striking the ball firmly on the green. A quick, clean sound that's all about control and precision. It's the auditory exclamation point on a confident putt, whether it's for birdie or bogey.

12. ***THLIT-THLIT.***
Ball skipping across a water hazard. A rare sound of fleeting hope. Those rapid little pings signal a chance—however slim—that your ball might make it to dry land. Or at least go down with flair.

13. ***DJOINK.***
Ball hitting the flagstick. The sound of hope colliding with destiny. Sometimes it's an almost-hole-out; other times it's a reminder that your aim was on, even if your power was a *little* off.

14. ***KUH-CHUNK.***
Clubface digging into and through rough or thick grass. A.k.a. the earthy sound of resistance overcome, it's the auditory embodiment of effort, and it lets you know that recovery shots are part of the game, too.

15. ***THWAINK.***
Ball dropping onto the base of a metal flagstick. Not quite the *doink* of hitting the stick, but just as satisfying in its own way. It's the ball saying, "I'm here," as it confirms its place on the green.

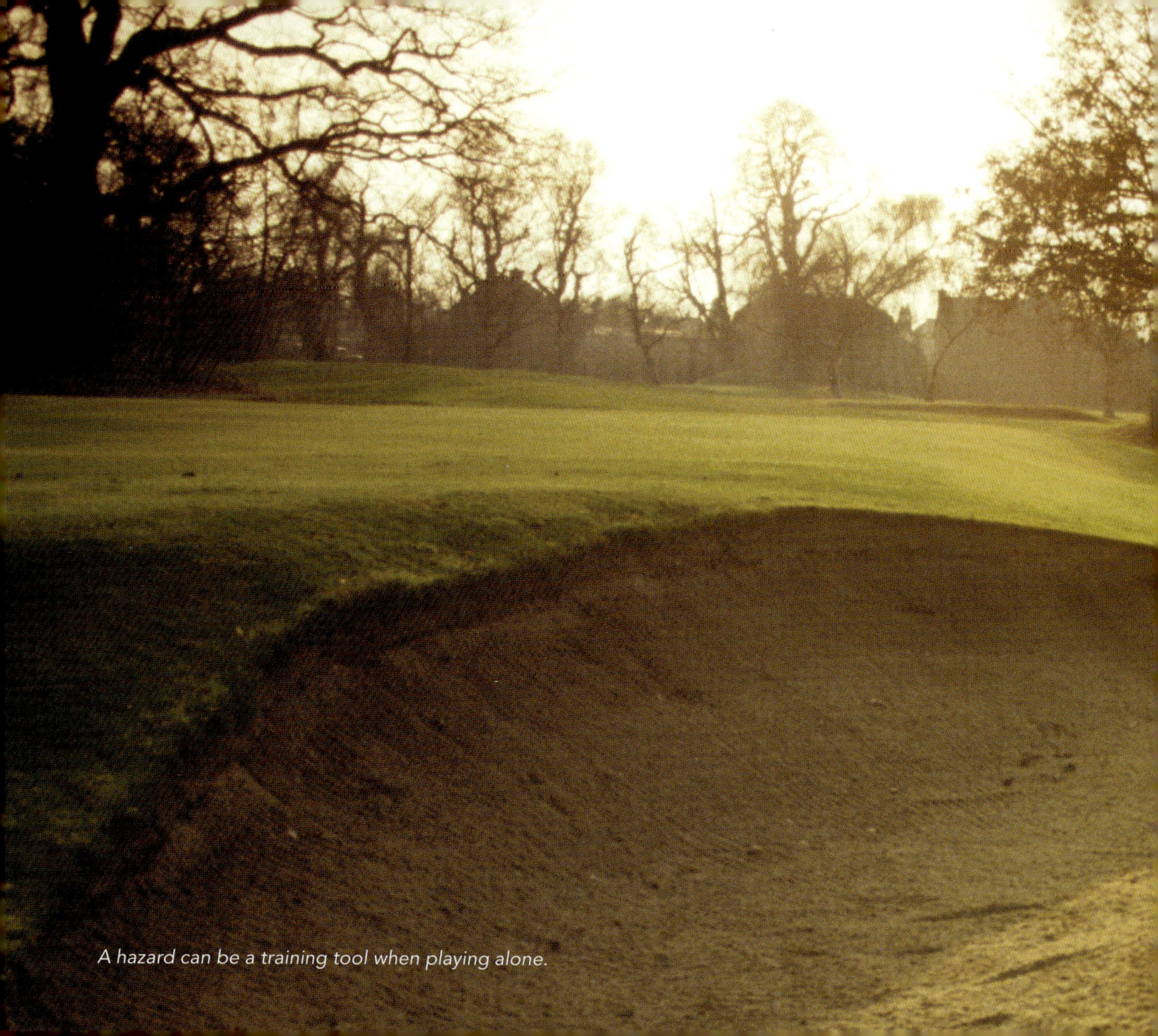

A hazard can be a training tool when playing alone.

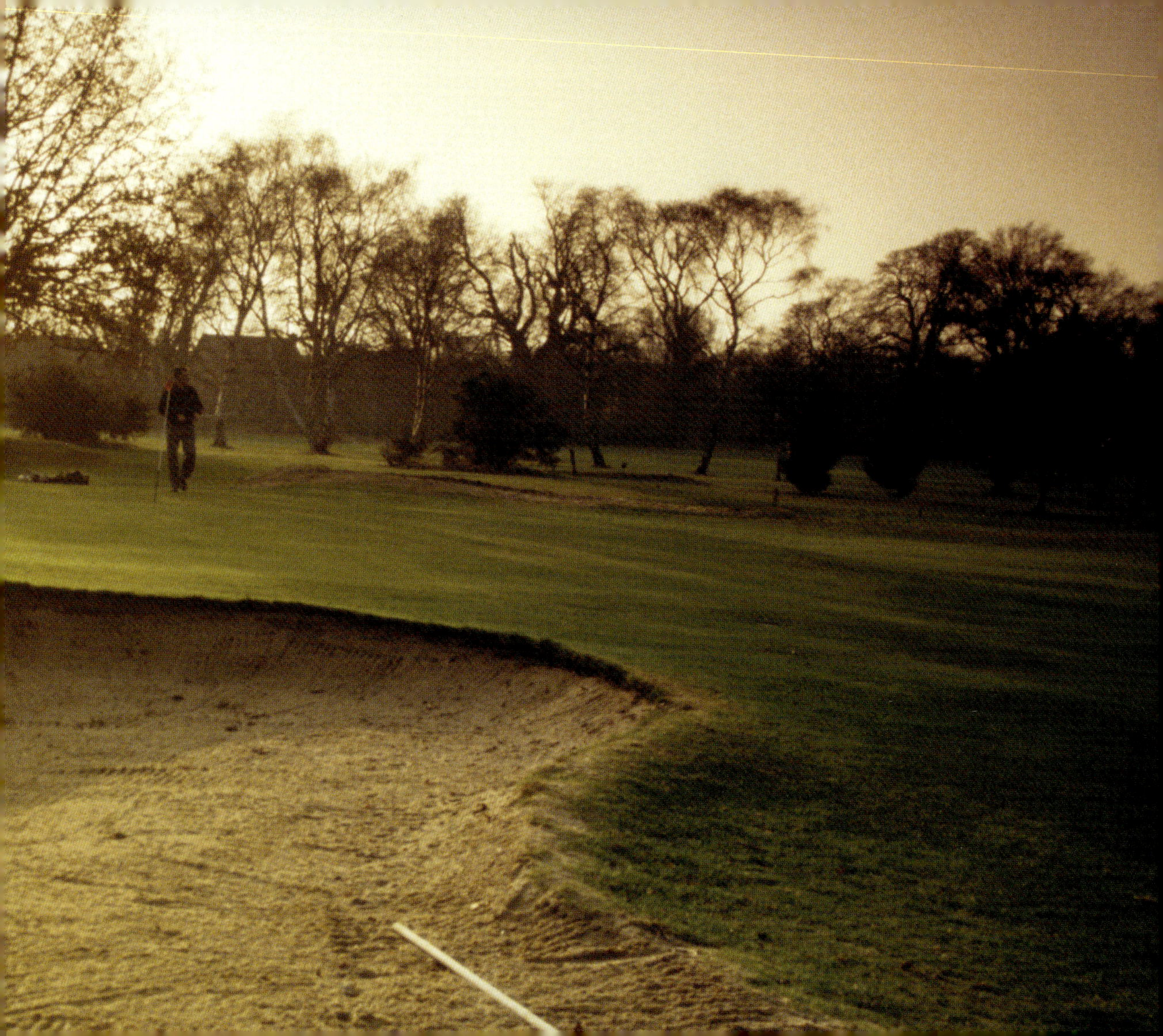

"Concentration comes out of a combination of confidence and hunger."

—ARNOLD PALMER, *golf legend*

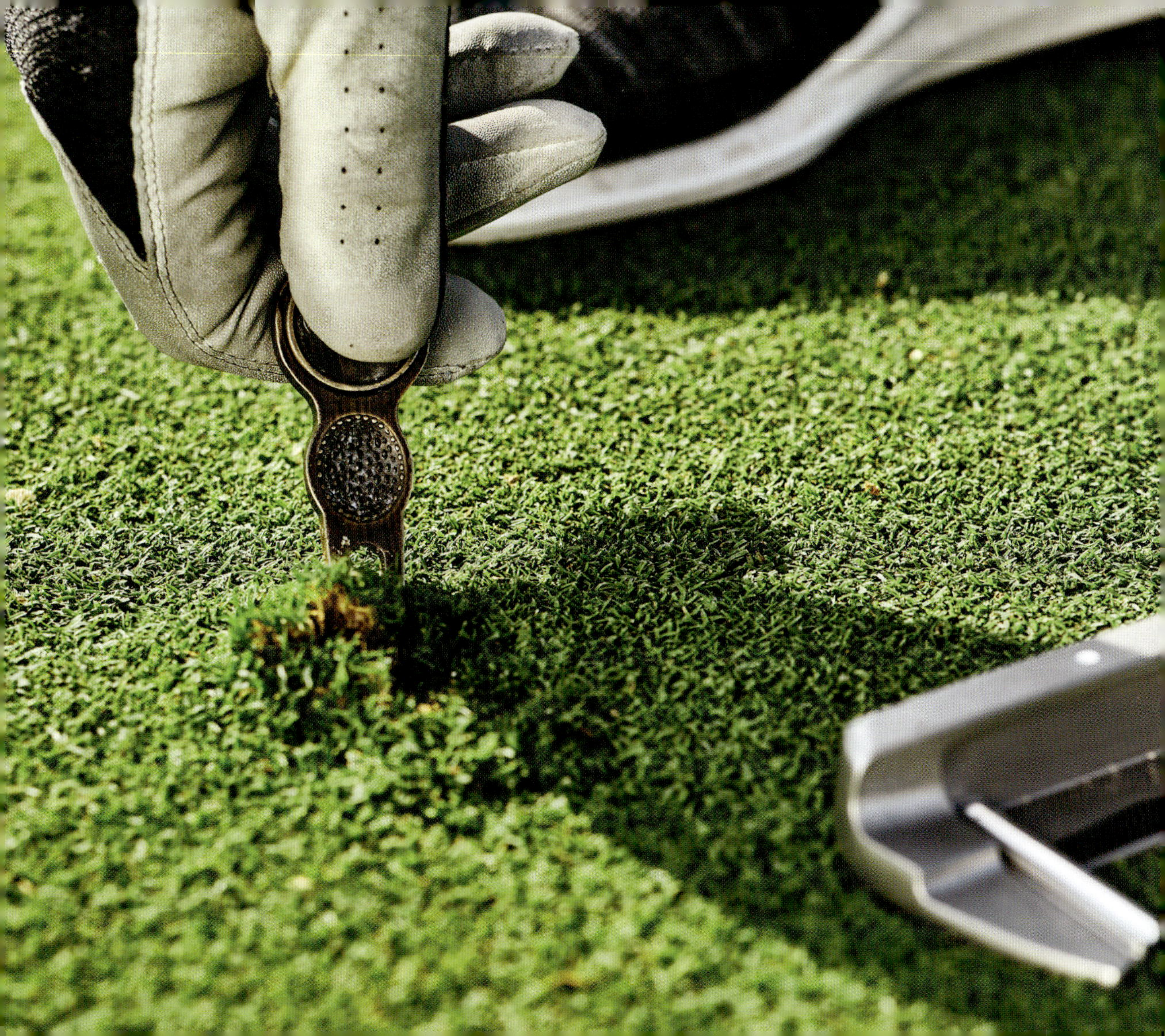

A Meditation on Focus

Many years ago, a mini-tour professional was playing a casual round of golf with a weekend hacker in the suburbs of New York City. Near the end of what was for him a challenging round, the amateur asked his playing partner a seemingly simple but incredibly profound question: "What is the single biggest difference between me and you?"

Both players understood that by "me" the amateur meant high-handicappers (a.k.a. weekend hackers) and by "you" he meant scratch golfers or better (a.k.a. people who could make a living at the sport) and by "difference" he meant on the golf course, not in life.

The pro's reply came quickly and had absolutely nothing to do with any of the dizzyingly numerous components of a single golf shot, i.e., club selection, grip, set-up, address, waggle, takeaway, downswing, hip turn, swing plane, club face angle, impact speed, release, follow-through, tempo, rhythm, or any other mechanical aspect of what might very well be the most overanalyzed, dissected, anatomized, and compartmentalized sport in the history of humankind.

In fact, the pro's response to the question had absolutely nothing whatsoever to do with the amateur's body or form.

"Oh, that's easy," he answered, with a smile that bordered on pitying. "When I'm standing over my ball, that particular shot is the only shot I'm thinking about at that particular moment. When you're standing over your ball, you're thinking about every other shot that's come before—in that particular round and probably in some others!"

It would be hard for anyone familiar with the average player's golf game to argue with that assessment. Golf is a mental challenge, an ongoing psychological battle between central purpose and irrelevant distractions. It is a sport that punishes overthinking yet rewards mindfulness, a seeming contradiction that defies logic but neatly defines the game's key to success.

In that way golf is different from most other commonly played or spectated sports. Think about it: When was the last time a professional baseball player asked for quiet from the crowd while facing the prospect of hitting a rock-hard ball speeding toward them at 90-plus mph from 60-plus feet away? Even in tennis, when etiquette calls for spectators to observe silently during service, there's no proscriptive against cheering loudly while 95 percent of a match's strokes are made.

Compare this reality with that of golf, when even the most focused professional will restart their pre-shot routine should a spectator so much as cough during their set-up. That's how challenging it can be to minimize distraction and maximize focus.

For amateurs, this challenge is compounded by never-ending internal chatter. It's not just an awareness of external distractions—a plane overhead, a rustle in the trees—but also the litany of self-criticism and second-guessing that can creep in: "Try to relax," or "You always top it with this club." These mental intrusions are relentless, and they're part of why golf is often described as a game played "six inches between the ears."

Except far less so during a solo round. Playing alone, solo golfers experience what can best be described as liberation, a joyful deliverance not only from the self-consciousness that comes from being watched as they hit but also from the myriad social obligations of the sport. Not having to chat up others *and* track their shots *and* hunt for their balls *and* discuss distances *and* keep their scores leaves most solo golfers with a heightened clarity of mind.

In the absence of social noise, the game becomes far more meditative. The stillness of the course, the steady cadence of your steps, and the rhythmic repetition of your swing create a mental environment where focus can flourish. It's not that distractions disappear entirely, but they no longer seem to matter. Without the need to perform for others, you can sink into the task at hand—one shot, one moment at a time.

As much as many golfers enjoy playing with friends, relatives, and (most) strangers, being part of a twosome, threesome, or foursome carries obligations and expectations. Solo golf, on the other hand, leaves room for a certain kind of selfishness, a chance to immerse oneself completely in the rhythms and pleasures of *your* game.

This immersion often leads to surprising discoveries about your own abilities. Freed from the pressure of keeping pace with others or living up to an imagined standard, you may find yourself taking risks you'd otherwise avoid, like trying a bold approach shot, experimenting with a new grip, or hitting a club you wouldn't normally trust. (And perhaps trying again if you fail.) These moments of unfiltered focus and exploration are where true growth happens, both as a golfer and as a person.

This kind of "me time" allows for easy introspection and nonjudgmental self-awareness, fostering a connection with the activity itself. The closest parallel might be in the kitchen. Although preparing meals with others offers its own kinds of pleasures, many chefs find cooking alone far more relaxing—and the results something to savor.

Ultimately, the focus you find in solo golf transcends the sport. It's a reminder of the power of presence, of giving yourself fully to a single moment. That lesson, learned on the fairway or green, can carry over into the rest of life. Because, in the end, aren't all the shots we take—on or off the course—best approached one at a time?

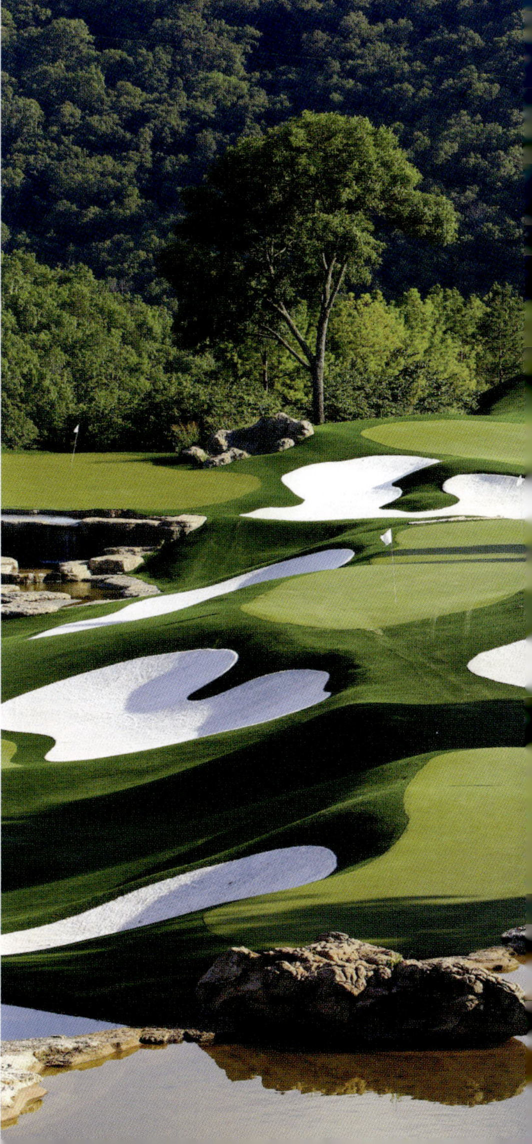

FOCUS-FRIENDLY ACTIVITIES

Respect routine.
Algorithms are everything. In golf, too. The more disciplined your pre-shot routine, the less there is to consider, allowing your mind to zero in on the task at hand. A well-practiced routine reduces distractions by creating a predictable sequence, almost like a mental checklist. Ritual steps may seem a little silly at first, but when you no longer have to think about them consciously, they transform into an automatic rhythm that builds confidence. Over time, these routines feel like pixie dust, seamlessly bridging preparation and execution.

Be present.
Avoid thinking about previous shots. Lingering frustration or pride over what's already happened can cloud your focus. If you find yourself replaying a previous shot in your head, gently redirect your attention back to the present by reestablishing your routine. Focusing on *this* shot, *this* swing, and *this* moment gives you the clarity to perform your best. But if you can't, notice it and redo the activity above.

Keep something—but only one thing—in mind.
Golf swings are notoriously complex. Thinking about every moving part—grip, stance, shoulder alignment, hip rotation—is a recipe for overload. Instead, isolate just *one* element to focus on during your swing. Maybe it's keeping your head still or maintaining a smooth tempo. Stick with that single thought until it becomes second nature, and only then shift to another focus area. This deliberate practice keeps your mental energy from being scattered and makes improvement more manageable.

Visualize your shot.
"See" what you want to happen before your backswing. Take a moment to mentally rehearse the outcome you want. Visualizing the ball's flight, trajectory, and landing spot creates a mental blueprint for success. This not only sharpens your focus but also primes your body to execute the shot as your mind has already "seen" it happen. Visualization is a proven tool used by athletes across sports for a reason—it works.

Smile.
No, seriously. It sounds too simple to be true, but smiling just before your backswing can work wonders. Smiling activates the parasympathetic nervous system, reducing stress and tension. This subtle shift helps clear your mind and puts you in a positive frame of mind, which is crucial for focus. Think of it as a quick reset button for your mental state.

Breathe.
Another "obvious" piece of advice that's more nuanced than you might think. Taking a deep breath—specifically in through your nose and out the same way, but slightly slower—has a calming effect. It centers you and brings your focus back to your body and the moment. Breathing this way just before your backswing can relax your muscles and reduce the chance of tension affecting your swing. If you find yourself tightening up, simply return to your breath.

Take mental breaks.
It's okay to think about what happened after a shot. You can learn something from it. But thinking is not obsessing. Walking between swings offers a natural opportunity to reset. Use this time to step away mentally—notice the scenery, listen to birds, or enjoy the solitude. Briefly thinking about non-golf topics can give your mind the rest it needs to stay sharp when it's time to focus again. Avoid obsessing over what went wrong; instead, think about what you've learned and let it go.

Use a mantra.
Repeating a simple word or phrase—such as *smooth*, *steady*, or *follow through*—can create a mental anchor. This mantra keeps your thoughts steady, reduces overthinking, and helps you maintain rhythm and consistency in your game.

Check your posture.
Body language influences mental state. Standing tall with a relaxed posture can subtly boost confidence and focus. Slouching or tension in your body can signal your brain to feel stressed. Before every swing, ensure your posture is intentional—calm but engaged.

Minimize environmental distractions.
Environmental factors can tug at your attention. Take a moment to scan your surroundings before stepping into your stance. Clear the area of anything that might pull your focus away: a stray twig, a distant siren, or even the rustle of wind through nearby trees. Pause for a moment and it might pass.

Hydrate and snack.
Mental focus is tied to physical well-being. Staying hydrated and eating a small snack, like a handful of nuts or a banana, can keep your energy and concentration levels steady throughout your round. Dehydration or hunger can make it harder to stay present, even if you're not immediately aware of it.

Practice gratitude.
Yeah, yeah, it sounds very New Age-y. Even so, take a moment before each shot to appreciate the solitude, the course, and the joy of playing. Gratitude can quiet negative thoughts and enhance focus by shifting your mindset to one of positivity and presence. You can even make it part of your pre-shot routine!

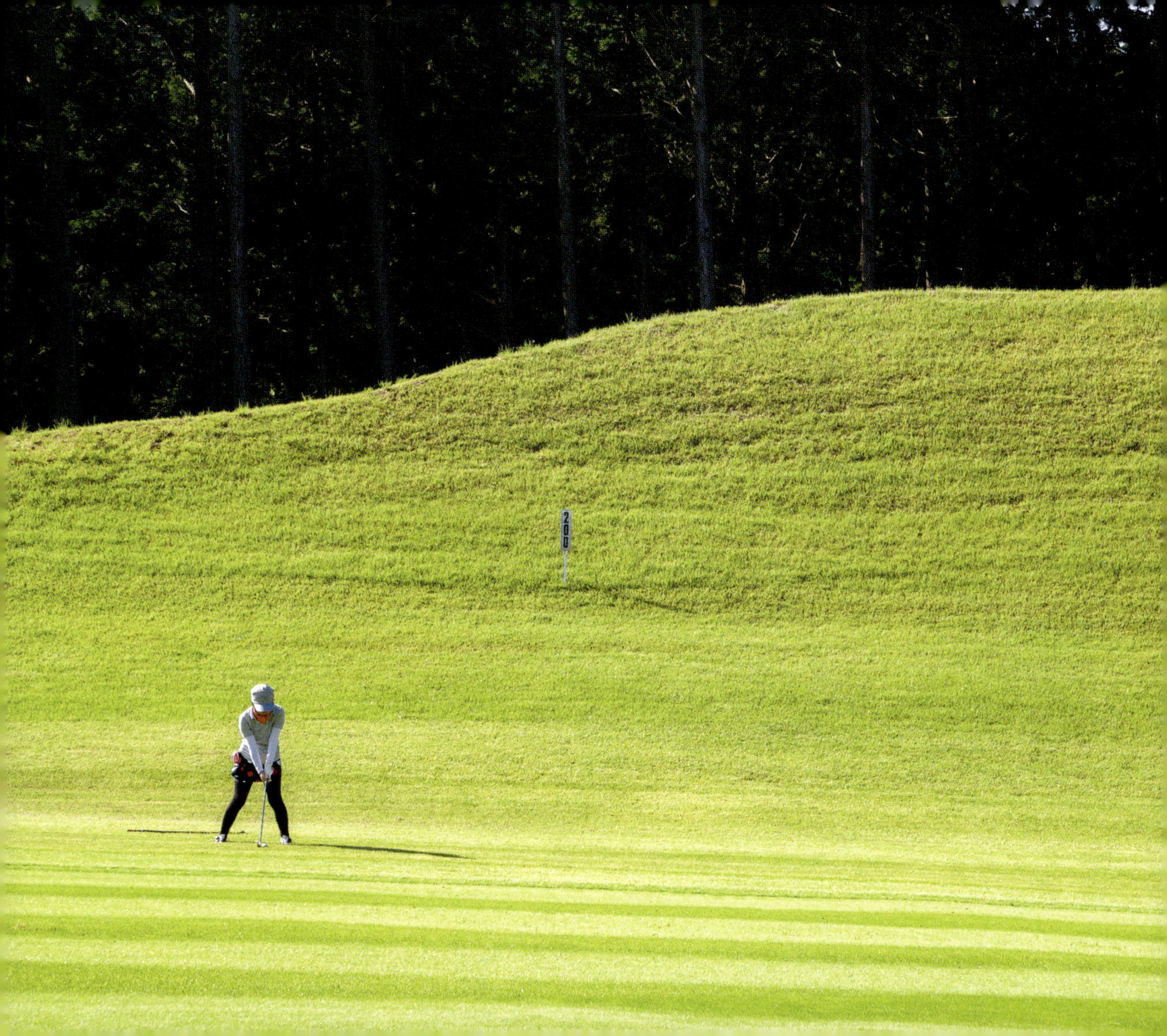
200

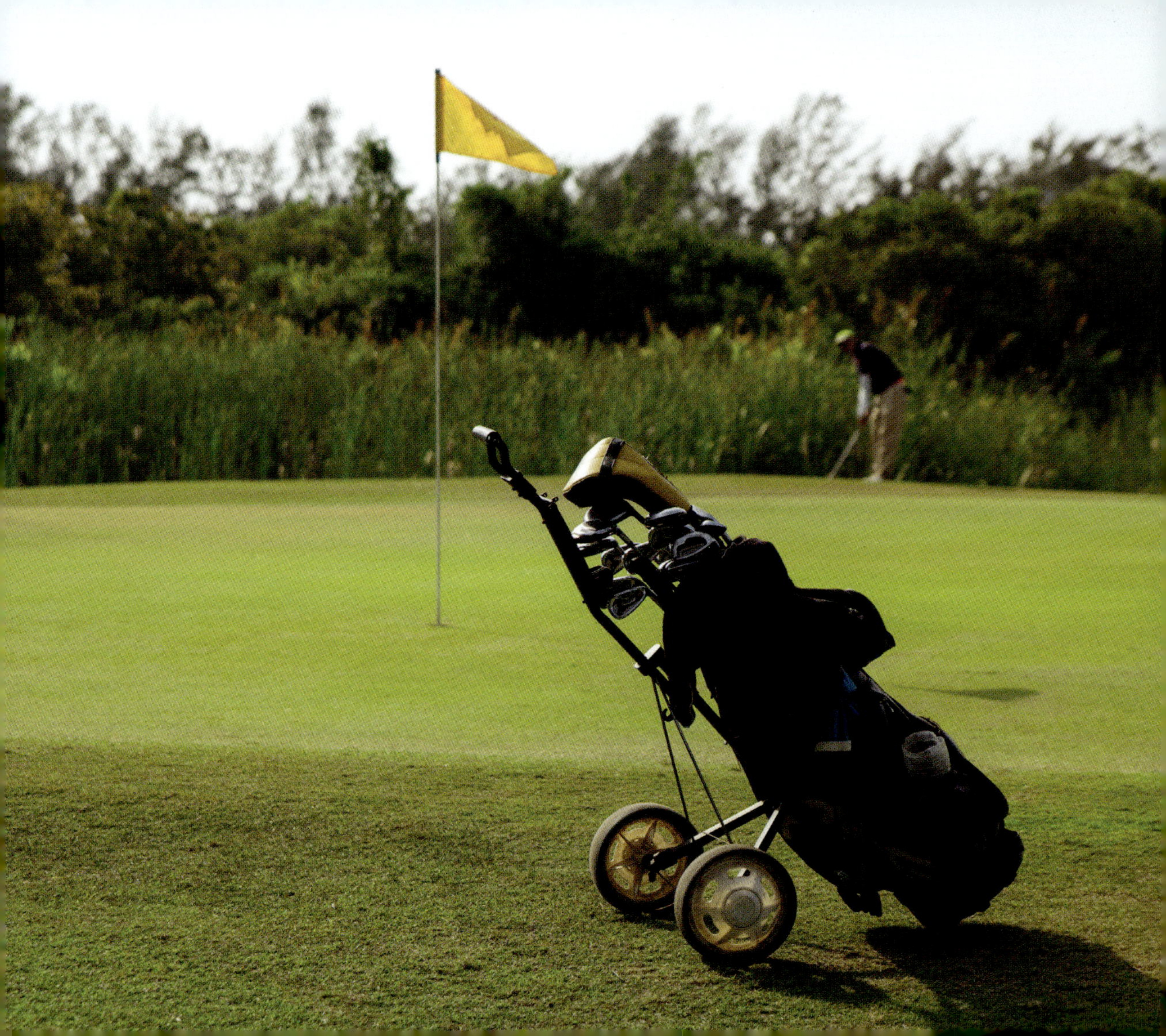

"A poor craftsman blames his tools."

—BRITISH IDIOM

A Meditation on "Things"

Siddhartha Gautama—a.k.a. the founder of Buddhism—was not, insofar as anyone knows, a golfer. But one of the fundamental principles in Buddhist philosophy is "non-attachment," a concept that requires practitioners to let go of their connection to and regard for material possessions (among many other things).

Which brings us to solo golf.

Although this book contains (I hope) helpful advice for planning meaningful alone time on a course, most of the solo rounds you will play—and many of the most enjoyable—will likely be the product of serendipitous decision-making. In fact, these excursions might very well come about when you're traveling for purposes other than playing golf, which will mean that you end up swinging rented or borrowed clubs (and wearing, if available, rented or borrowed shoes).

For some, this might sound like a compromise or even a recipe for disaster, but it's actually a hidden blessing. Playing with unfamiliar equipment pushes you outside of your comfort zone and forces you to focus on the fundamentals of the game—your stance, your swing, your rhythm—rather than relying on the fine-tuned characteristics of your own clubs.

What's notable about all this is that matters of equipment reveal something fundamental to the nature of many, if not most, amateur golfers. A large proportion of them spend many hundreds or thousands of dollars—on multiple occasions—buying clubs, which they then proceed to talk about as if they are their children or pieces of fine art.

In other words, golfers love their clubs. Always have and always will—right up until the moment they decide that it's time for a new set (or at least a new driver/putter/hybrid).

And yet . . .

For all of your investment—literal and metaphorical—in the tools of the sport, you will likely find the experience of playing with clubs that aren't yours freeing. There's an undeniable charm in the unpredictability of borrowed or rented equipment. A driver that doesn't quite fit your grip or a set of irons with a slightly different weight distribution can force you to adapt, and, in doing so, you'll rediscover the core of your swing—the part of you that's unencumbered by muscle memory or technological crutches.

There's something exciting, even a little dangerous, about teeing off with a strange driver or putting with someone else's short stick. It's like adultery without the guilt—or expectations.

This sense of adventure often carries over into how you approach the game itself. You might find yourself more willing to try a risky shot or experiment with a different strategy, because, after all, these aren't your clubs. It's as though the borrowed equipment gives you permission to play more freely, without the burden of perfection that often accompanies the familiar.

That last note, more likely than not, is the reason why many of the best holes and rounds of a golfer's life will occur when they have played alone. That's not because they're making scores up for the benefit of subsequent storytelling. Nor does it result from the absence of competition (and witnesses), which inherently lowers the stakes of any shot, hole, or round. Rather, it is because when we borrow or rent someone else's equipment, we concomitantly acquire the most legitimate of excuses for below-average performance—*I'm not playing with my own clubs*—which can, ironically, lead to above-average performance. The entire exercise, in other words, is a preordered mulligan, an outing's worth of relaxed practice swings, with no downside and a genuine shot at golfing nirvana.

And perhaps that's the ultimate lesson here: that golf, stripped of its trappings, rituals, and material things, is at its heart a simple game of striking a ball and enjoying where it takes you. Borrowed clubs remind you of this truth. They take away the noise of ownership and replace it with a quiet freedom—the kind that solo golf is meant to inspire.

THINGS YOU CAN RENT AT THE COURSE	THINGS YOU CAN'T RENT AT THE COURSE
Clubs	Shirts
Carts	Shorts
Shoes	Socks
Range Balls	Regulation Balls
Beer	Skill
Playing Partners	Actual Friends

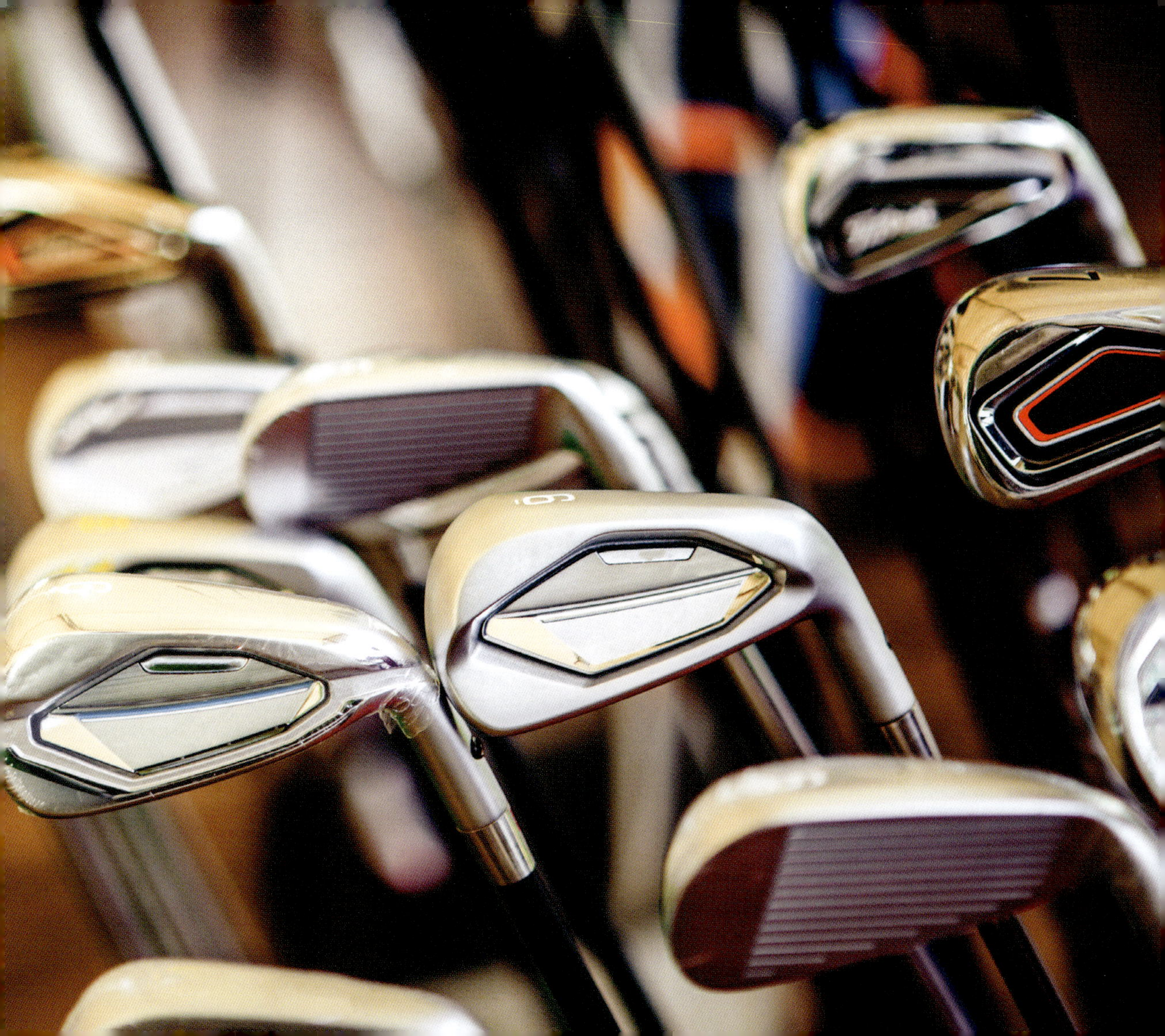

"People will often miss out on learning because they're afraid to fail in public. But playing alone they'll try something they wouldn't if someone else was there. And through that they start to build confidence."

—MOLLY BRAID, *PGA Professional*

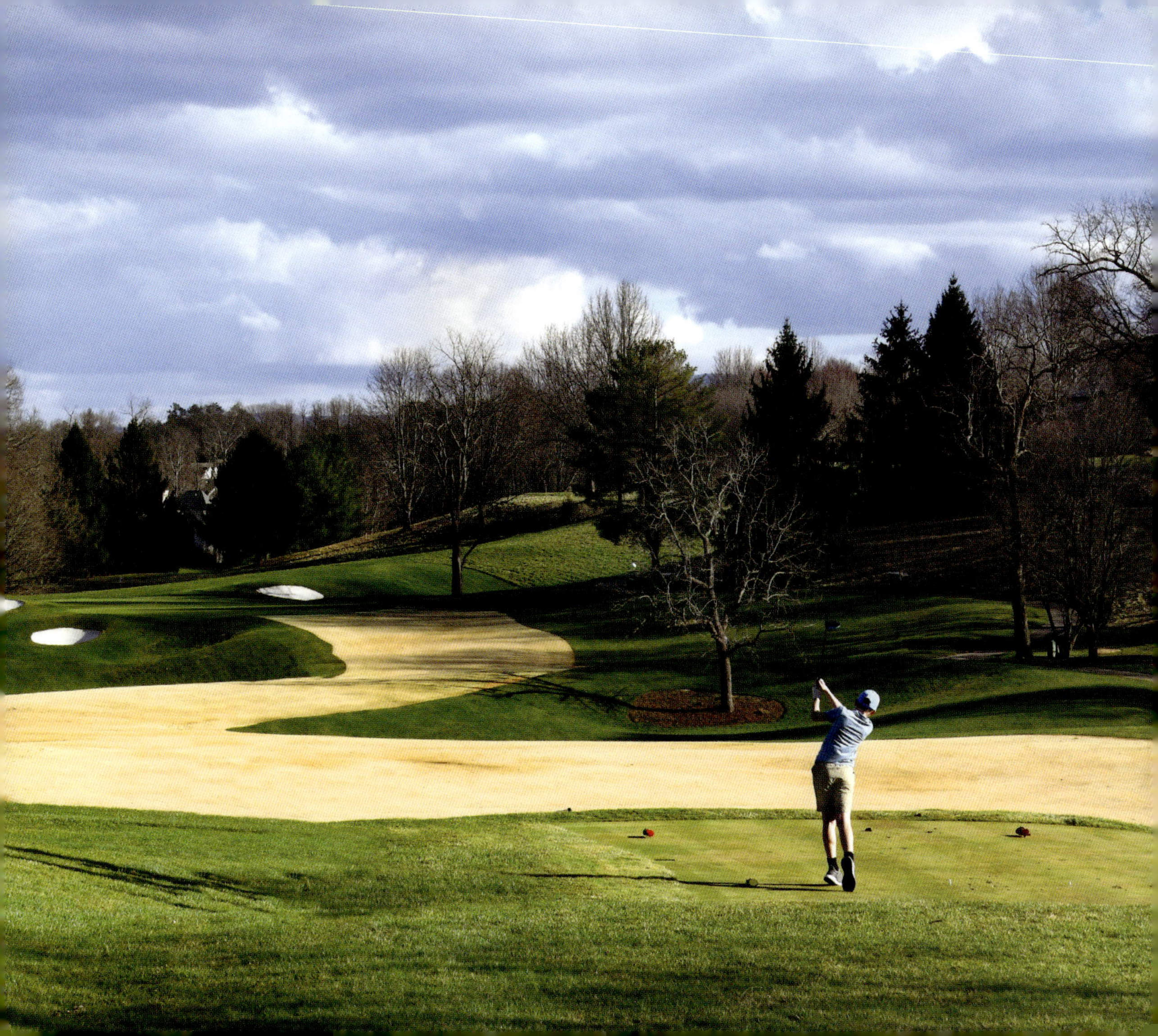

A Meditation on Perspective

If [fill in the sport] is a game of inches, then golf is a game of millimeters. Although the practical gulf between the best and the rest is expansive, the numerical separation is relatively minuscule. Consider this synopsis of that reality, which is as true today as it was when first noted during the prime competitive years of Tiger Woods:

- If you average 73 strokes per round, you'll be the most popular playing partner at your home course.
- If you average 72, you can attend college for free on an athletic scholarship.
- If you average 71, you can make a living as a professional golfer.
- If you average 70, you'll be a millionaire.
- If you average 69, you'll be a multimillionaire.
- And if you average 68, well, you'll be the most famous person in the world.

Yes, the difference between good and great in golf is both wider and slimmer than most ordinary people genuinely understand.

The realization of this truth can change the way one approaches the game. For many golfers, there comes a moment of reckoning—whether it's triggered by a conversation with a playing partner, an especially humbling round, or plain old self-awareness—when they recognize that perfection is neither attainable nor required. This shift in perspective can make the game infinitely more enjoyable.

You, too, may have found yourself taking the game too seriously: talking to yourself, overanalyzing club selection, or fixating on wind conditions as if each and every variable may hold the key to your success. While striving for improvement is part of the sport's appeal, there's a fine line between ambition and obsession. If you've ever crossed that line, you know how it can drain the joy out of what should ultimately be a recreational activity.

One of the great lessons golf can teach is to embrace the game's inherent imperfections, as well as one's own. Once you let go of the need to "fix" everything and instead focus on enjoying the process, you may discover a whole new level of fun. This is especially true during solo rounds, where the absence of spectators or playing partners frees you from self-consciousness and opens the door to experimentation.

Which brings us to the real point of this chapter: An underrated aspect of solo golf, one that rarely gets mentioned by coaches or on Reddit or in similar forums, is the opportunity to be silly.

Silliness in this context isn't about being frivolous; it's about giving yourself permission to explore the game in unconventional ways. Solo golf creates

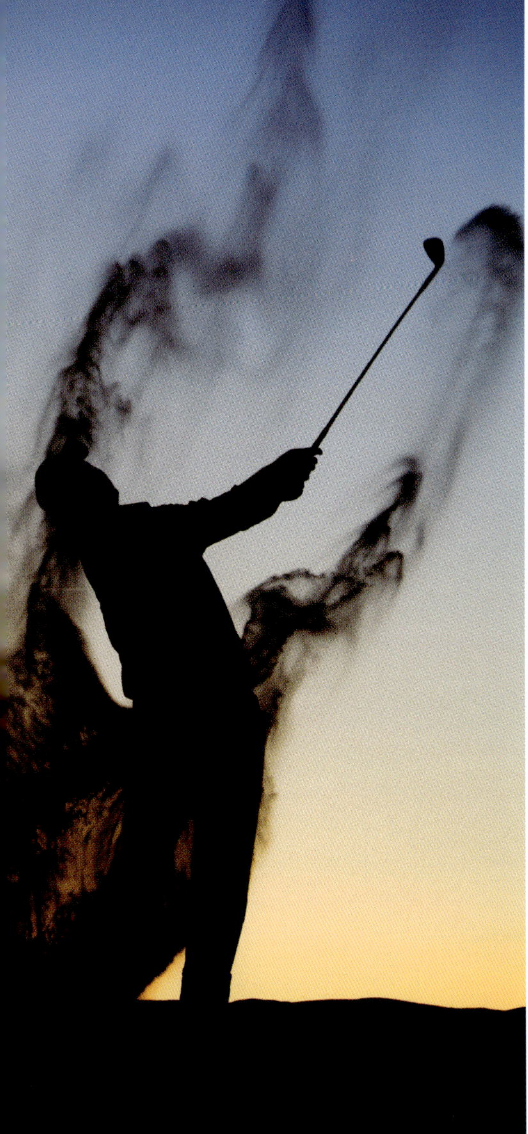

a space where you can play on your own terms, unrestricted by social norms, group dynamics, or self-consciousness.

Imagine standing alone on the tee box with no one watching, no one waiting, and no one to judge. You can pretty much do whatever you want out there, as long as it doesn't harm the course or slow play. Have you ever thought about playing a hole with only a putter? You can try it, testing your precision and creativity. What about using a driver for every shot, from tee to green to cup? Or playing a green as though you're in a pool hall, using your putter like a cue stick?

You might even try "soccer golf," kicking the ball the length of a hole. (Pro tip from your author: Stick to par-3s for this and remove your shoe when you get to the green—no one wants to chunk up the surface.) Or "handball golf," throwing the ball the length of a hole. (Again, par-3s are best, and you'll quickly discover that mastering the right throwing techniques for different distances is its own challenge.)

These little experiments add a layer of playfulness to the game. They remind you that golf doesn't always have to be about scorecards and handicaps. It can be about curiosity, inventiveness, and sheer enjoyment.

To be clear, silly golf is different from using a solo round as a laboratory for improving your game (see Part II). You'll likely play most of the holes in most of your solo rounds as traditionally as any other golfer might. But every once in a while, when a whimsical thought strikes, you have the freedom to follow it to its natural expression on the course.

Do some of these wild-hair ideas fall flat? Of course. Not every experiment is a success. But the ones that work often bring a level of joy and spontaneity that's hard to replicate in group play. And, occasionally, you may discover something worth sharing—a quirky challenge or variation that's even more fun with others, especially if a friendly wager is involved.

The key takeaway is this: Golf is meant to be fun, and solo golf is an excellent opportunity to rediscover that truth.

You may not remember every score or every shot from your solo rounds, but the moments when you allowed yourself to let go, laugh, and play will stick with you. These are the memories that remind you why you fell in love with the game.

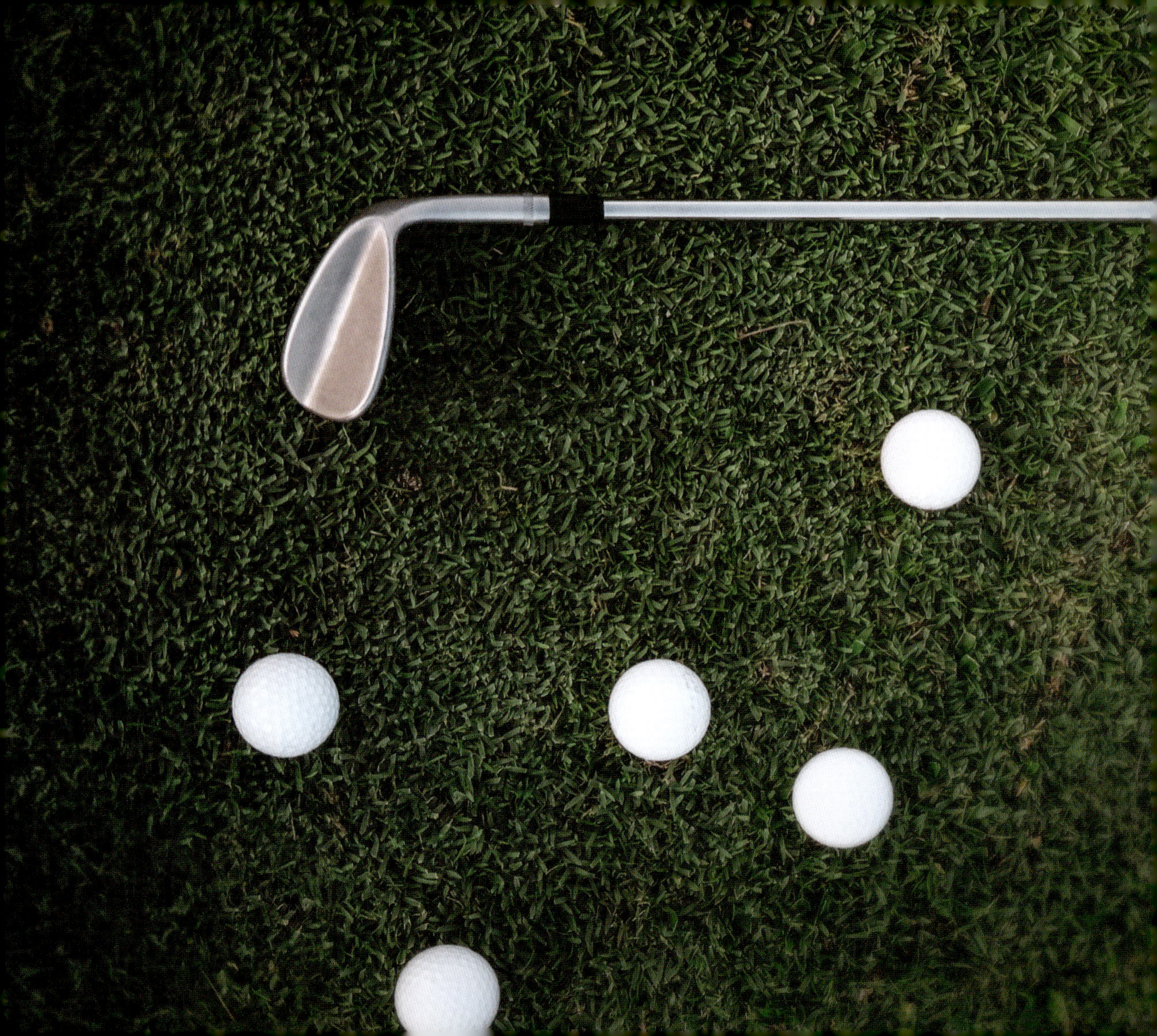

THE 10 GREATEST (AND SILLIEST) SONGS ABOUT GOLF

Feel free to load these onto a playlist for your next solo round.

1. "Straight Down the Middle" (Bing Crosby)
2. "Hit It Hard" (John Daly)
3. "18 Holes" (John Denver)
4. "Double Bogey Blues" (Mickey Jones)
5. "I Love to Play" (Jake Trout & the Flounders)
6. "Golf Girl" (Richard Sinclair)
7. "That Golf Song" (Duff Daddy)
8. "Shitty Golfer" (Toby Keith)
9. "Chase the Fairway" (Bård Vassbø Jr.)
10. "Keep It in the Short Grass" (Bob Galindo Jr.)

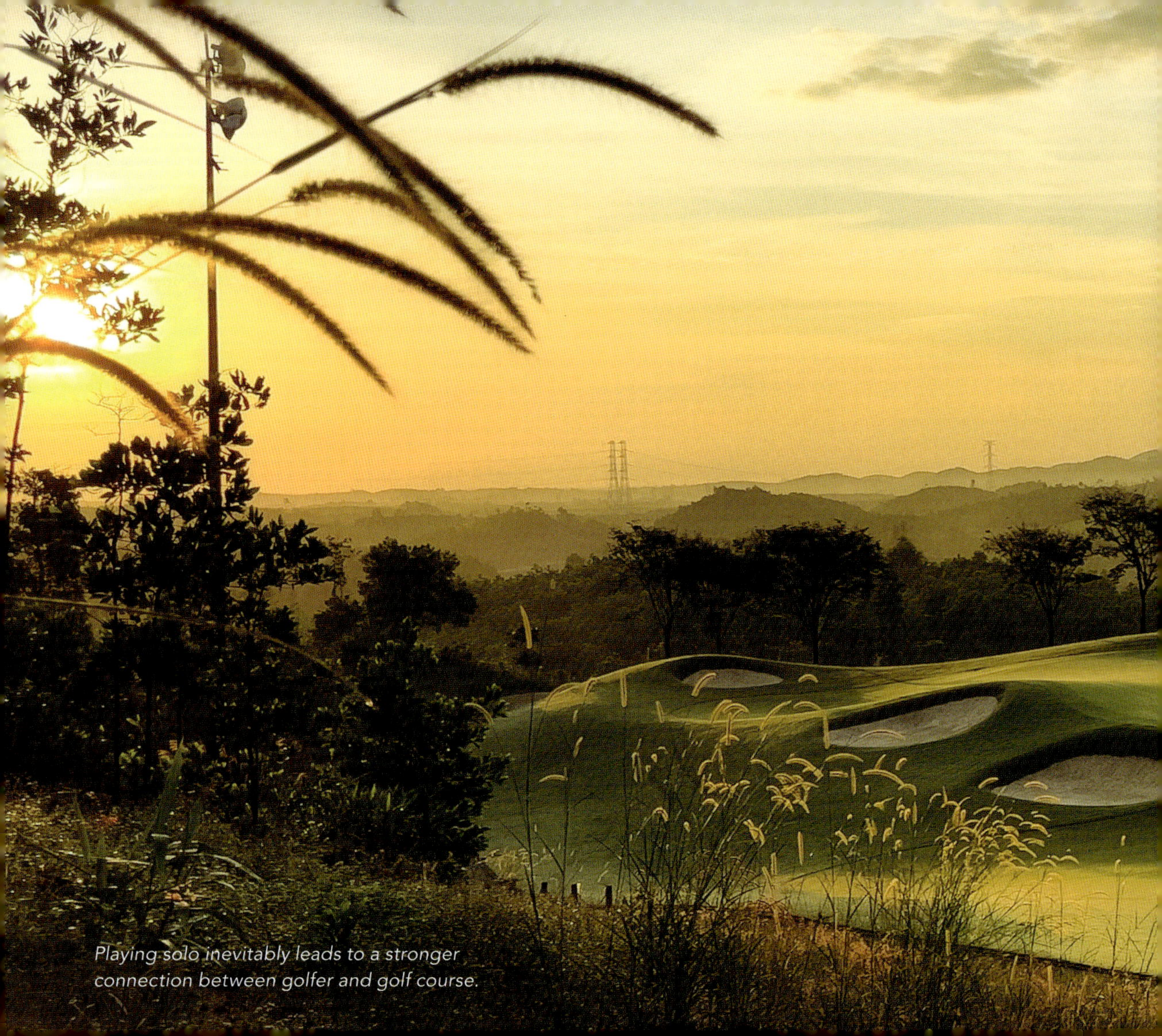

Playing solo inevitably leads to a stronger connection between golfer and golf course.

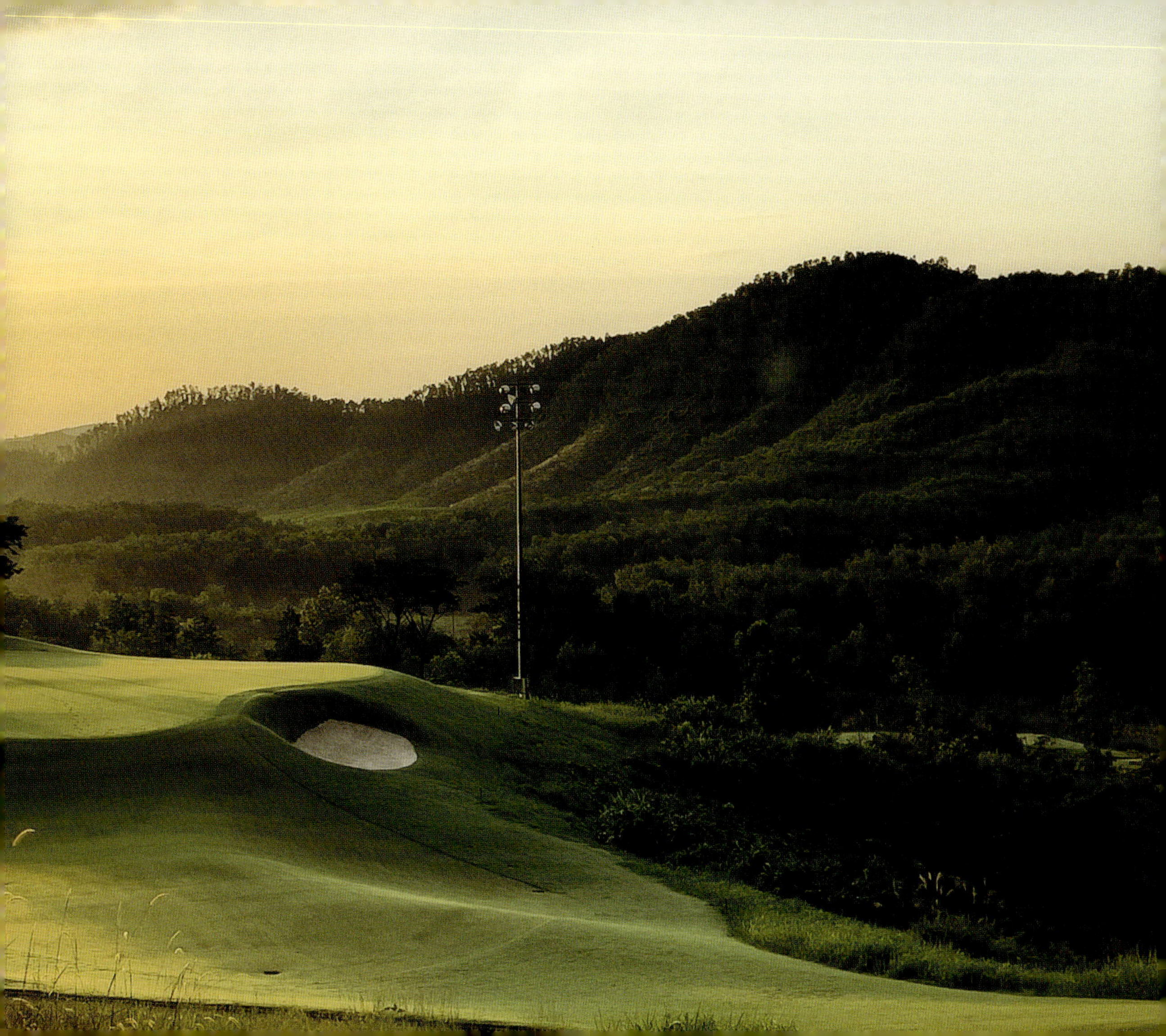

"If you truly love golf, you must love the fact that no one shoots 50, that golf is an inherently imperfect game. If you spend your time fighting the fact that golf is a game of mistakes and trying to make it a game of perfect shots, you're really saying that you don't like golf."

—BOB ROTELLA,

sports psychologist

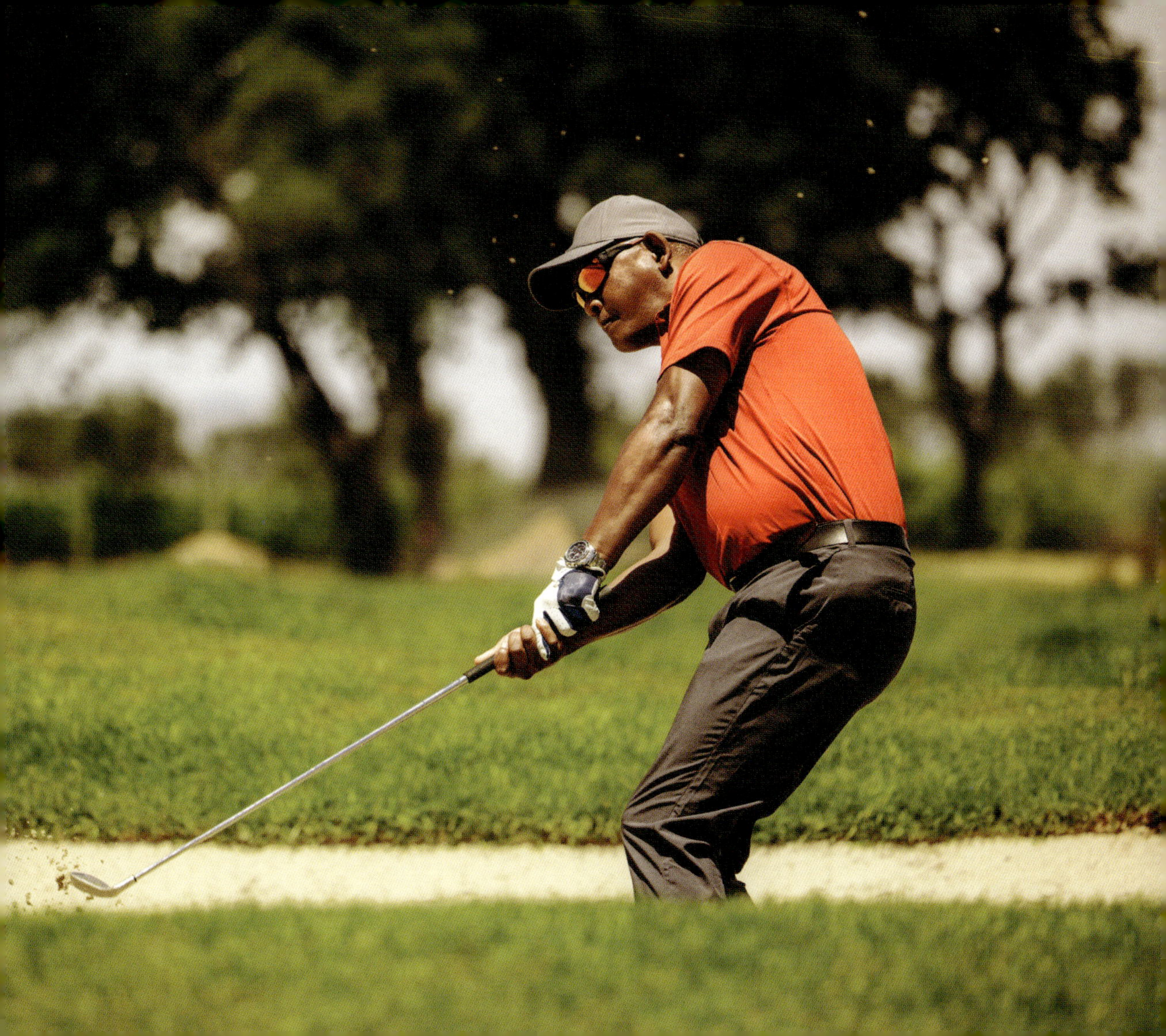

A Meditation on Self-Acceptance

It's often surprising how intimate and personal solo golf can feel, even to those who love talking about the game. For many, solo rounds are a quiet, private affair, a stark contrast to the camaraderie and storytelling that often define group play. You might notice that, unlike other athletic pursuits or social rounds, you rarely discuss your solo golf experiences with others. It's not because they're less meaningful—in fact, the opposite may be true. They're simply different, more interiorized, and less about external validation.

This contrast becomes even clearer when you think about how people approach other sports or hobbies. Most athletes, casual or competitive, are eager to relive their highlights. Consider how often people recount the diving catch they made in a beer league softball game or the clutch three-pointer they sank during a pickup basketball run. Sharing these stories is part of the fun, a way of connecting with others and reliving moments of triumph. And golfers are no exception—after all, recounting your sweet shots and bad breaks is practically a tradition in the clubhouse after a round.

But solo golf is different. It's quieter, more introspective. When you play alone, the highlights are just for you. There's no audience to applaud your 90-yard wedge that lands near the flag, no playing partner to witness the chip-in from the fringe. And yet, those moments can feel even more satisfying precisely because they belong solely to you.

There's a key parallel here to other solitary pursuits, like weight lifting. Both activities are deeply personal measures of your abilities and limitations. Psychologists often distinguish between intrinsic (internal) and extrinsic (external) motivation, and solo golf leans heavily into the former. When you're on the course alone, it's not about proving anything to anyone else. It's about your own connection to the game, your ability to focus, and the quiet pride you feel in accomplishing something, even if no one else is watching.

This shift in focus—from external validation to internal satisfaction—can be transformative. For example, in a group round, it's hard not to look up after a great shot to see if anyone else noticed. The cheers, compliments, or even nods of approval add to the moment. But when you hit that perfect drive or sink that tricky putt while playing solo, the satisfaction you feel is undiminished. In fact, it might even be heightened. Why? Because it's entirely yours. You don't need anyone else to affirm it.

Self-acceptance plays a central role here. When you're playing alone, you're free from the subtle pressures of group dynamics—the need to impress, the fear of being judged, the comparisons to others. Solo golf gives you the space to accept yourself as you are, flaws and all. A bad shot doesn't feel like a public failure; it's simply an interesting development or a challenge to overcome. Similarly, a great shot isn't about earning praise; it's about proving to yourself that you're capable, a feeling of satisfaction more than elation.

This perspective often extends beyond the course. Learning to appreciate your successes and forgive your mistakes in a solo round can teach you to do the same in other areas of life. It's a practice in self-compassion, a reminder that growth and fulfillment come from within, not from external accolades.

Another unique aspect of solo golf is how it highlights the importance of being present. Without the distractions of group conversation or the rhythm of others' games, you can fully immerse yourself in the moment. You notice the details: the sound of club striking ball, the arc of its flight, the way it lands and rolls. These small moments, often overlooked in group play, take on a profound significance when you're alone. They remind you of the beauty and simplicity of the game, unclouded by external noise.

In solo golf, every shot is yours alone to experience and observe, from the great ones to the awful ones, and everything in between: bombs, ropes, burners, hooks, shanks, slices, tops, chunks, whiffs, dinks, doinks, worm burners, tree knockers, chili dips, sand blasters, banana balls . . . well, you get the point. And more to that point: There is something momentously freeing about personal privacy. When you're not worried about what others think—when your game is a private practice along the lines of yoga, meditation, or tai chi—you can experiment, take risks, and play without fear of judgment. You can hit a flop shot over a bunker just because it feels right, or try a tricky punch shot under a tree simply to see if you can pull it off, or attempt a putt from 100 yards off the green because you've always wanted to. Success or failure, one-off or game-changer, it's all part of the solo golf experience, and it's all yours.

Ultimately, the beauty of solo golf lies in its simplicity. It's not about proving anything or meeting anyone else's expectations. It's about connecting with the game on your own terms, embracing the challenges, and celebrating the victories—no matter how small. And in that quiet, personal space, you might just find a deeper appreciation for both the game and yourself.

The key to solo golf isn't perfection; it's acceptance. That means being fully engaged in the moment but accepting whatever comes—and finding joy in the process. And in those moments of self-acceptance, you might just discover a game that has more to teach you than you realized.

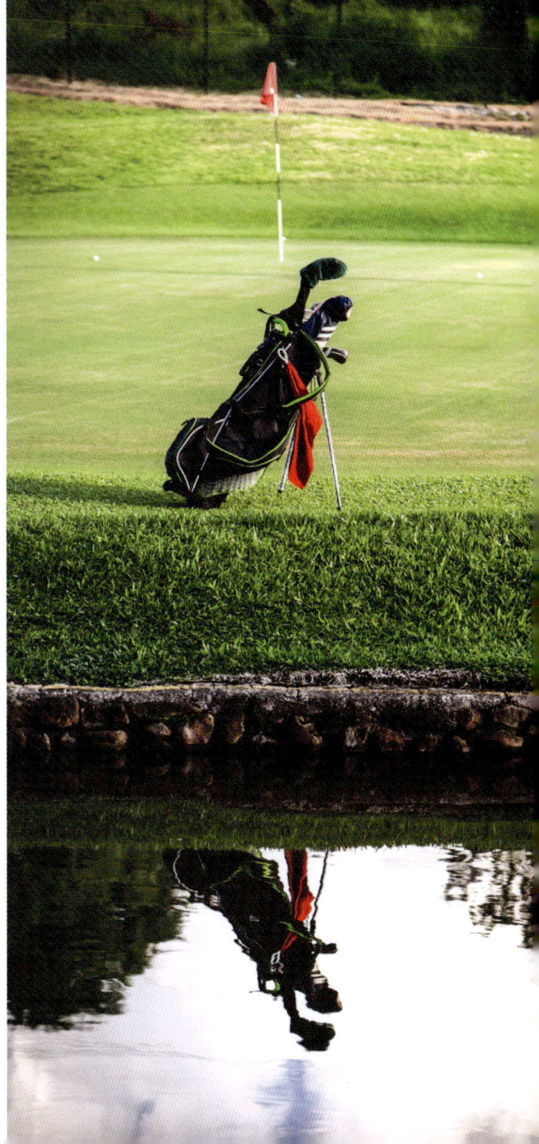

IF A SOLO GOLF BIRDIE TRY FALLS IN A HOLE, DOES IT COUNT TOWARD YOUR HANDICAP?

The short answer to this question: No.

The slightly longer answer: Still no, and it's all about how handicapping works. Handicapping, of course, is the system that makes it possible for golfers of varying skill levels to compete against each other. There's an intricate methodology to it—codified globally since 2020 in the World Handicap System—but the gist is that a player submits their score after a round, noting the difficulty of that particular course and tee placement (as measured by that course's official "rating" and "slope").

Scores go into a computerized database and—after 54 holes—a player receives an official handicap, which is then updated with each new posted score. Roughly 15 million golfers worldwide have official handicaps, and one-fifth of them are in the United States.

The lower the handicap number, the better the golfer—the range is from 0 to 54, for men and women—but the system's genius is to make that not matter very much. Any two handicaps can compete on a leveled playing field. So if a 2-handicap golfer and an 18-handicap golfer both shoot par on, say, the fifth-easiest hole of a course, the lesser-skilled player would win the hole because they "get" a stroke on each of the course's 18 holes, while the better golfer merits that benefit only on the two toughest holes (a 54-handicap golfer receives three strokes per hole).

One's handicap score has all sorts of meaningful consequences, from pairings in pursed tournaments to payoffs from "friendly" wagers. Indeed, in many instances golfers would prefer a handicap number that suggests a lower level of skill than they actually possess, the better to position them for scores that "surprise" and lead to a trophy or big financial payoff.

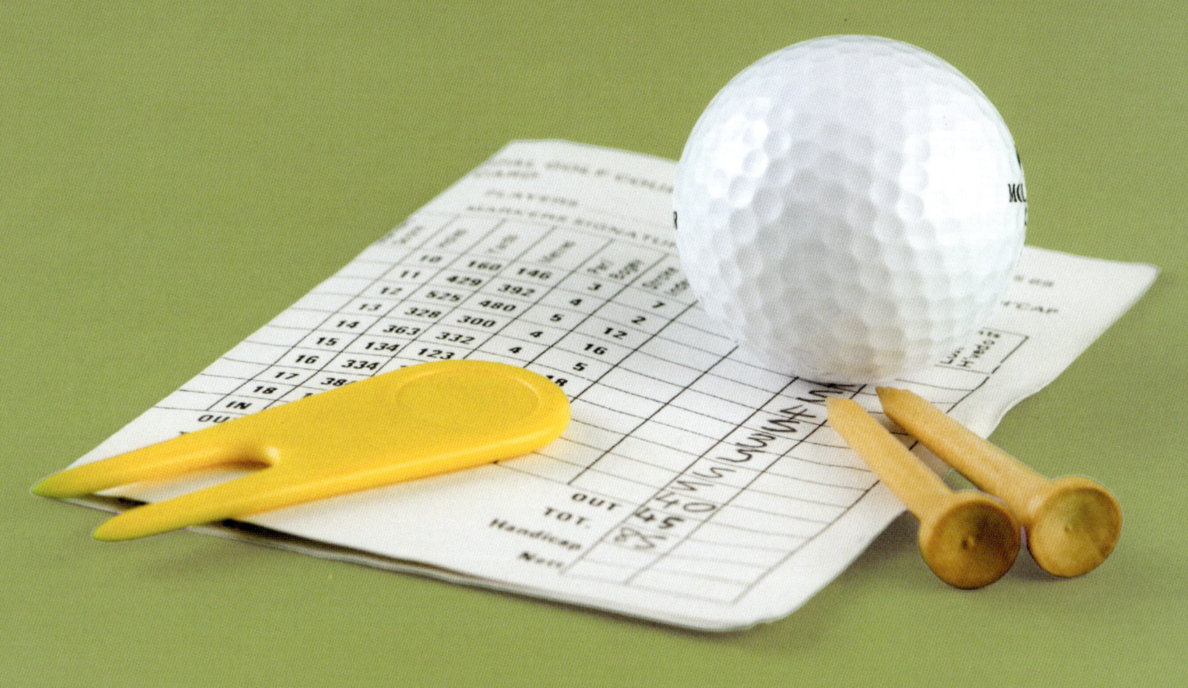

Which is why, despite golf's famous emphasis on player integrity, the official Rules of Golf stipulate, "A score is acceptable for handicap purposes if the round has been played . . . in the company of at least one other person."

Interestingly, that person can be a spouse, friend, or caddie who isn't playing. But if you are truly alone on the course—and even if you make a personal vow always to tally strokes with a CPA's rigor and a clergyperson's integrity—it just wouldn't be right for solo golf scores to count toward one's handicap.

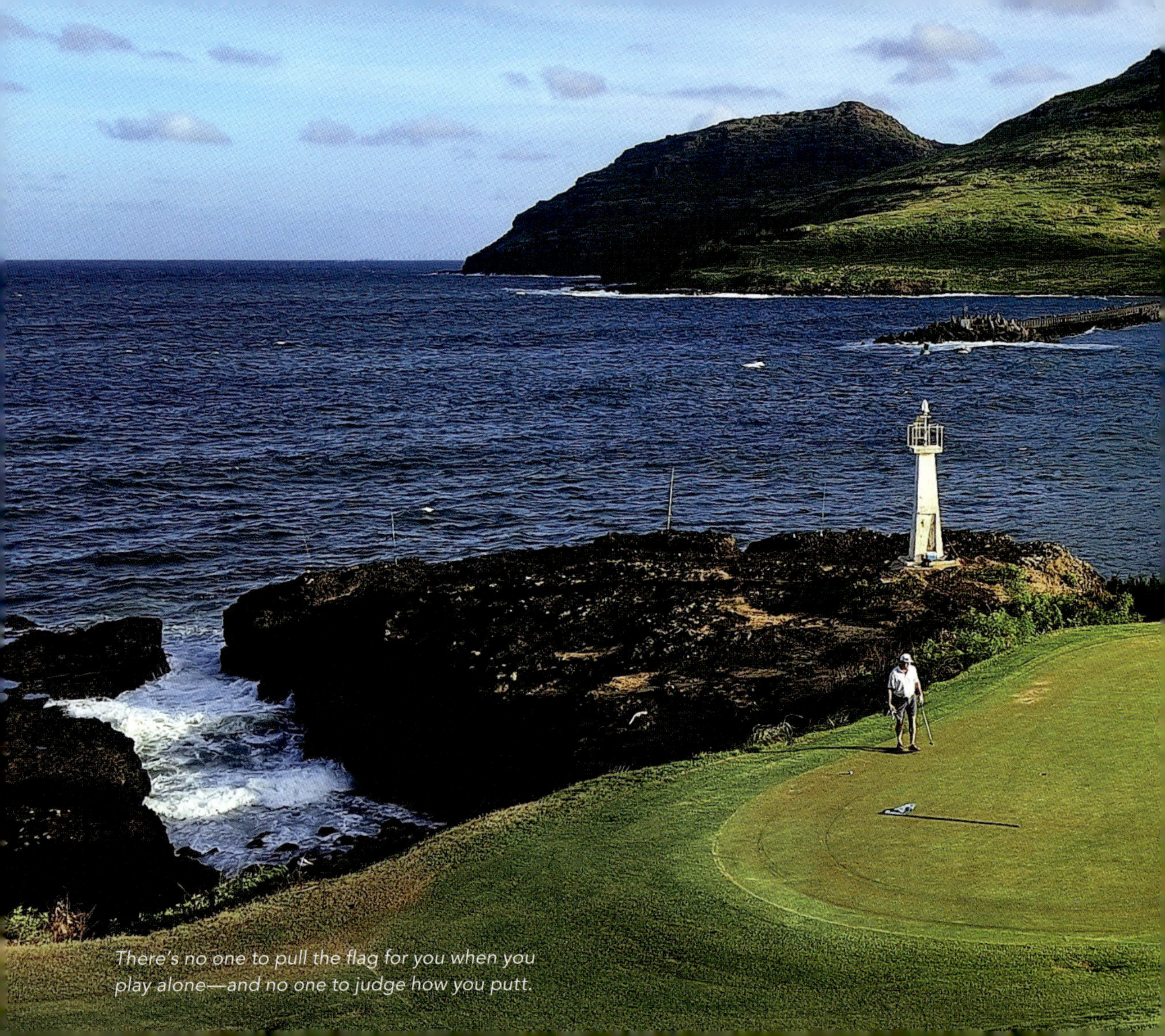

There's no one to pull the flag for you when you play alone—and no one to judge how you putt.

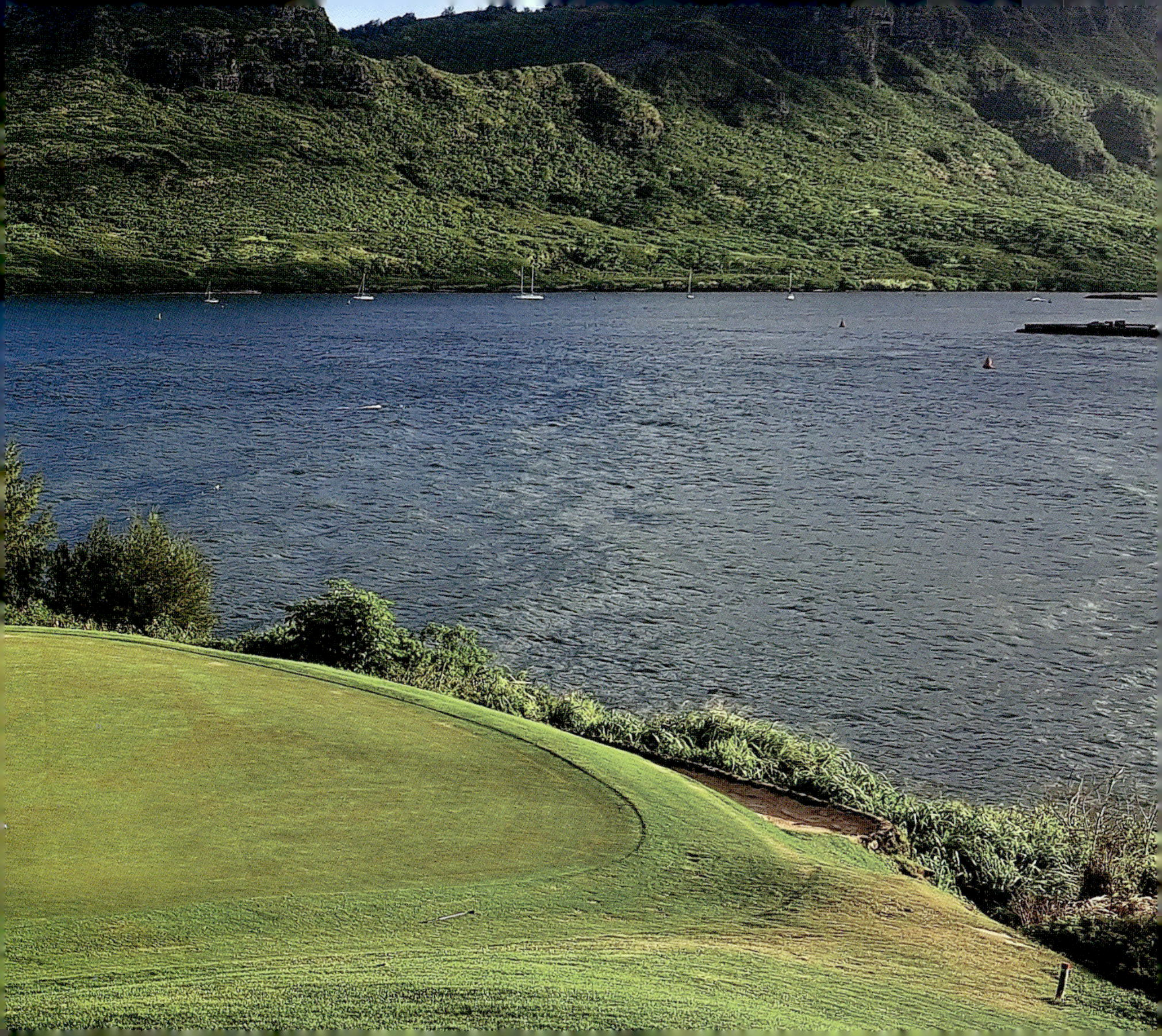

"Golf appeals to the idiot in us—and the child."

—JOHN UPDIKE,

Pulitzer Prize–winning novelist

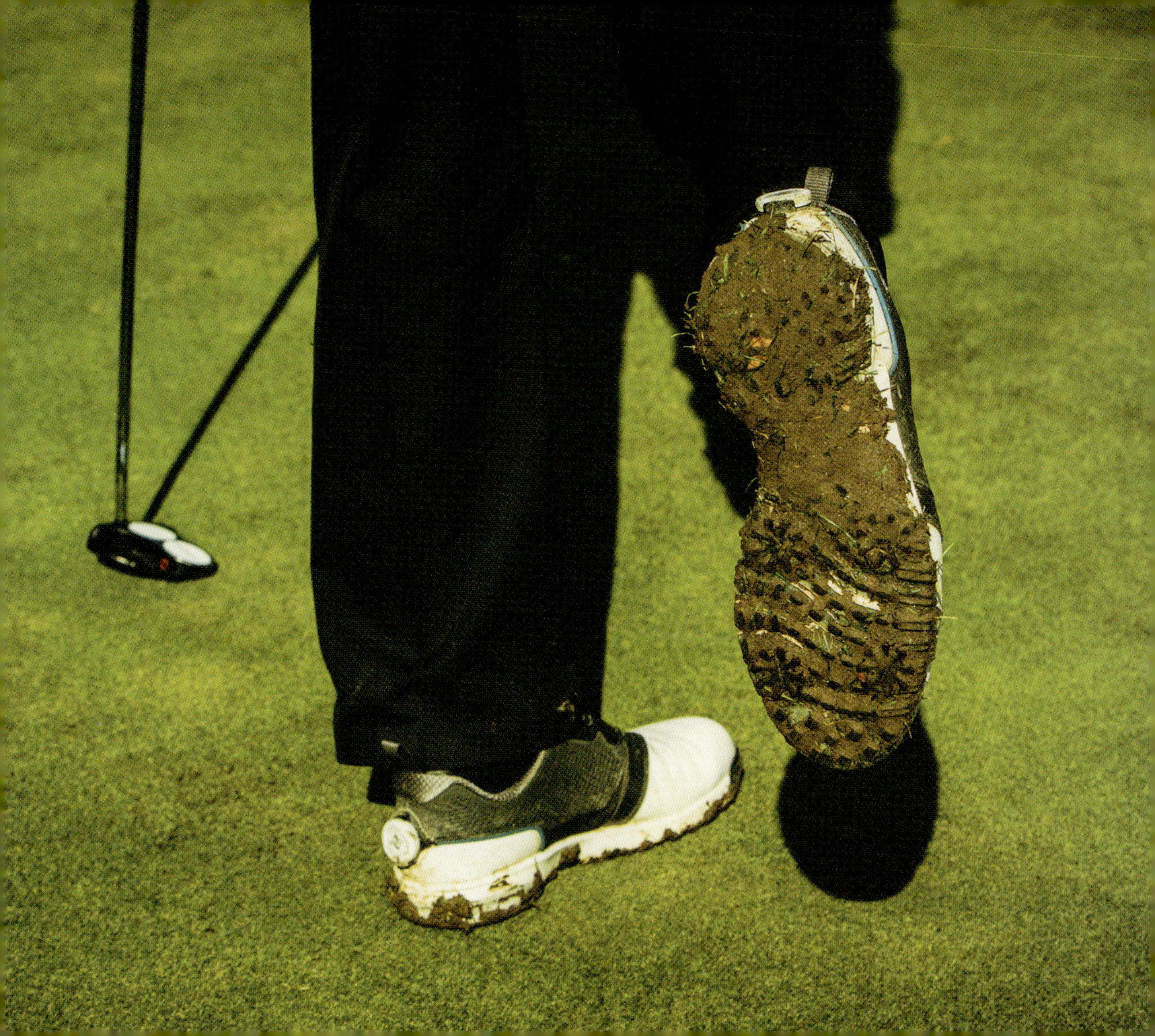

A Meditation on Imagination

"This crowd has gone deathly silent, the Cinderella story, outta nowhere, a former greenskeeper now about to become the Masters champion. It looks like a mirac—it's in the hole!"
—Carl Spackler, *Caddyshack* (1980)

Even if *Caddyshack* is not on your list of best golf movies (see page 66), Bill Murray's "Cinderella story" monologue from the iconic comedy is pretty much the archetype of a phenomenon unique to sports: the "play-by-play fantasy." For some it might start with something like, "Bases loaded, two outs in the bottom of the ninth, the Dodgers trail by three runs." For others it might be along the lines of "Fourth and goal on the one-yard line with three seconds on the clock, the Cardinals down by five." For still others, especially if they're from somewhere other than the United States, it might be one last corner kick in the World Cup Final stoppage time to beat Brazil.

But regardless of the scenario specifics, participatory sports provide a rare opportunity for genuine childlike fantasy (regardless of one's age). And such clutch-moment daydreams are more easily given full-throated expression—and are far less likely to generate friendly mocking—when one is alone on a driveway hoop bombing three-pointers in the last seconds of the seventh game of the NBA Finals than playing a pickup game with other adult humans at the gym.

Solo golf is no different. It provides a delightful opportunity for the imagination to take center stage, free of the constraints of reality and social expectations. You can stand on the tee box and transform a routine par-4 into the 72nd hole of a major championship, the crowd roaring in your mind as you prepare for a pivotal shot. It doesn't matter that the only spectators are a few sparrows or a squirrel perched on a branch. In your head, you're under the brightest lights and facing the highest stakes.

The point being, solo golf is good for the soul for one final reason: It offers the freedom to let your inner child run wild, to put yourself in a storybook spotlight, under make-believe pressure, or in the company of imagined greatness. And whatever your individual flight of fancy might be, there's real benefit to be gained from finding time in your life for daydreaming.

A growing body of research suggests that engaging in such vivid, immersive daydreams can improve physical well-being, strengthen mental health, and boost creativity. When you imagine yourself sinking a birdie putt on the 18th green at Pebble or blasting a long iron from the rough to within feet of the pin at Royal Troon, you're doing more than just playing a game—you're tapping into a wellspring of cognitive and emotional benefits.

This kind of thing isn't for everyone, of course. But daydreaming during solo golf allows you to break free from the mundane, helping to shift your perspective and turn an ordinary round into an extraordinary narrative. These moments of mental storytelling can serve as a form of escapism, offering relief from the pressures of daily life while also encouraging a sense of playfulness that's often missing from adulthood.

One of the beautiful things about solo golf is how seamlessly it accommodates these mental meanderings. Unlike other sports or group activities, there's no one else to remind you to hurry up or question the imaginary scenario you've concocted. Solo rounds give you the gift of time—time to savor the possibilities, to linger over a putt as if the world depends on it, or to stand over a bunker shot imagining it's the defining moment of your career.

Even beyond the big, dramatic fantasies, solo golf encourages smaller, quieter acts of imagination. Perhaps you visualize the exact trajectory of your shot, watching it in your mind before it takes flight. Or maybe you create mini challenges for yourself, pretending that a tricky up-and-down is for par, even if it's your fourth shot on a par-3. These mental exercises not only make the game more engaging but also sharpen your focus and deepen your connection to each shot.

And the beauty of it all? There's no judgment, no critique, no need to explain. Your imagination is yours alone, and solo golf provides the perfect canvas to explore it.

If those aren't good enough reasons to picture yourself sinking a 20-foot birdie putt late Sunday afternoon on the 18th green at Augusta, well, it's hard to imagine what might be.

The Pebble Beach of the mind: A vivid imagination means you don't really have to play alone when you play alone.

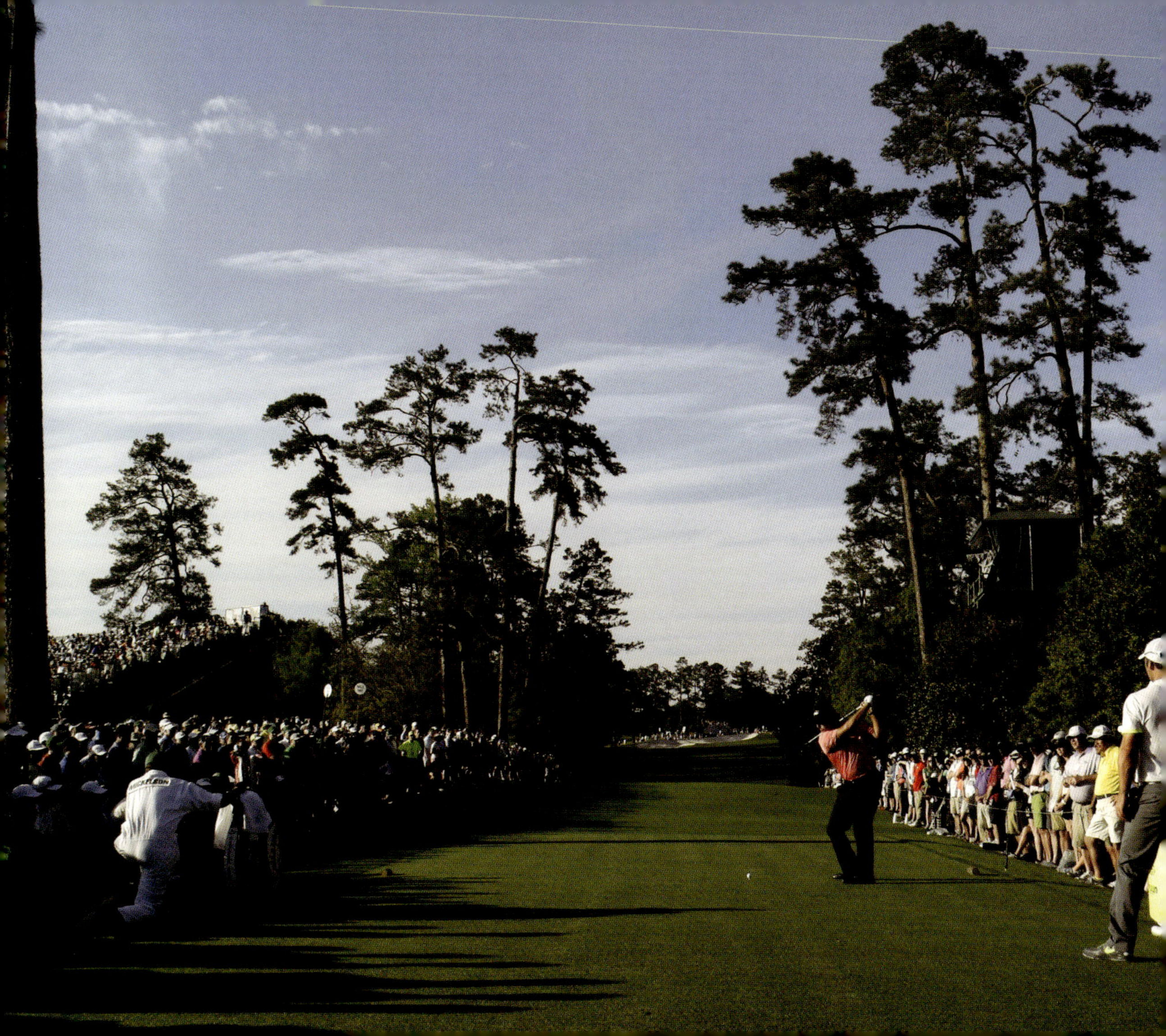

THE 10 GREATEST GOLF MOVIES OF ALL TIME

1. *Caddyshack* (1980). The golf and the plot are unconvincing, but the comedy stylings of a young Bill Murray & Co. make this a classic.
2. *Tin Cup* (1996). Kevin Costner loses the tournament of his dreams but finds the love of his life.
3. *Happy Gilmore* (1996). Adam Sandler turns the golf world upside down.
4. *The Phantom of the Open* (2021). There once was a very strange and not very good U.S. Open golfer—and this is his story.
5. *The Greatest Game Ever Played* (2005). There once was an against-the-odds U.S. Open champion—and this is his story.
6. *The Caddy* (1953). The greatest comedy (and crooning) duo of their era (Jerry Lewis, Dean Martin) wreak havoc on the golf course.
7. *The Short Game* (2013). A documentary about the U.S. Kids Golf World Championship.
8. *Pat and Mike* (1952). Two famous actors (and lovers) of their era (Spencer Tracy, Katharine Hepburn) take on sports corruption.
9. *Tommy's Honour* (2016). An insightful biopic about an early golf father-and-son dynasty.
10. *The Legend of Bagger Vance* (2000). Will Smith helps Matt Damon get his golf mojo back.

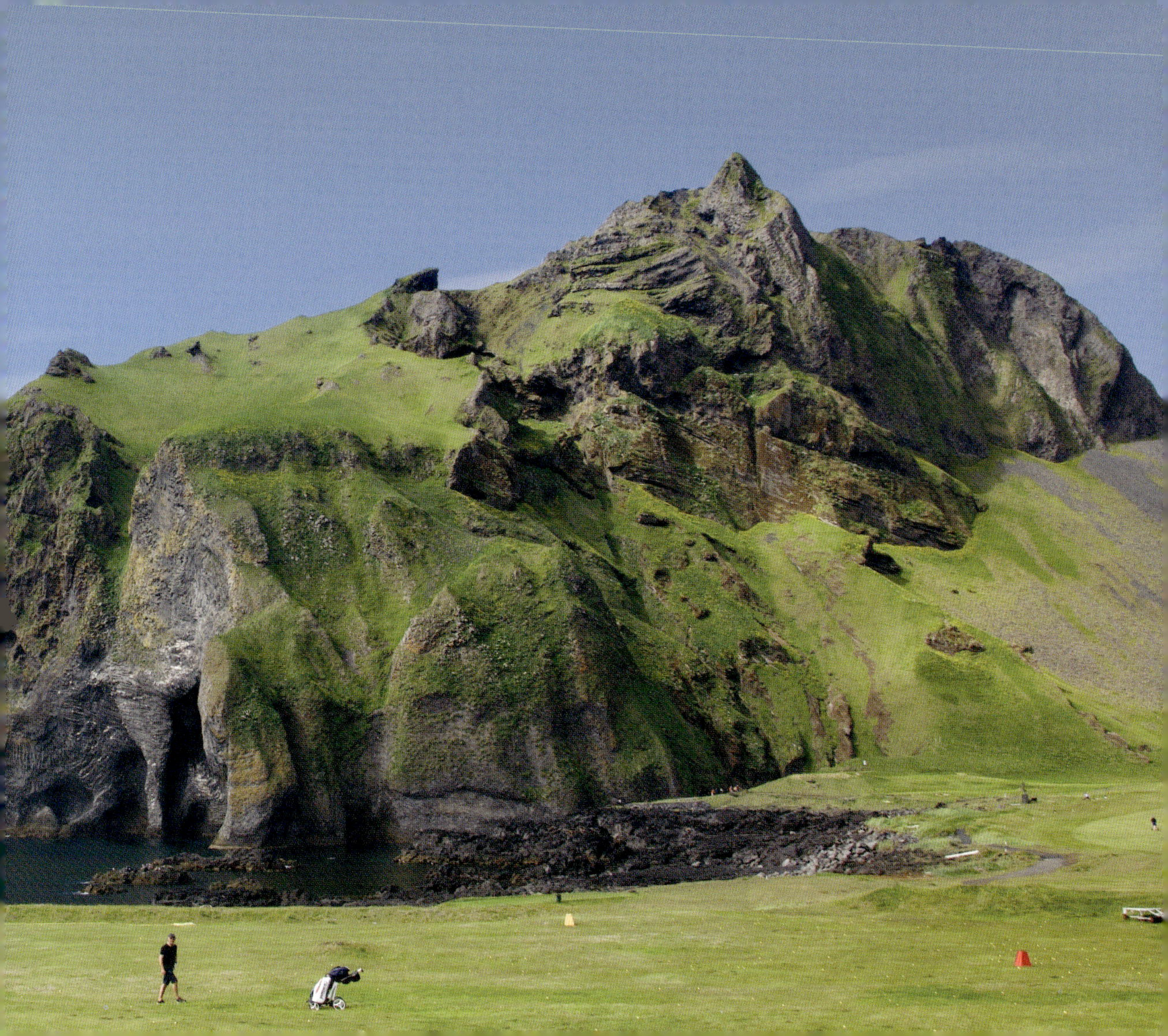

PART II

THE EXPERIMENTAL

Playing alone grants a kind of creative license that's hard to find in a foursome. This section is about using that freedom—to test clubs, replay shots, bend rules, and invent your own ways of navigating the course. It's not a matter of breaking the game; it's about deepening your relationship to it, one unsupervised experiment at a time.

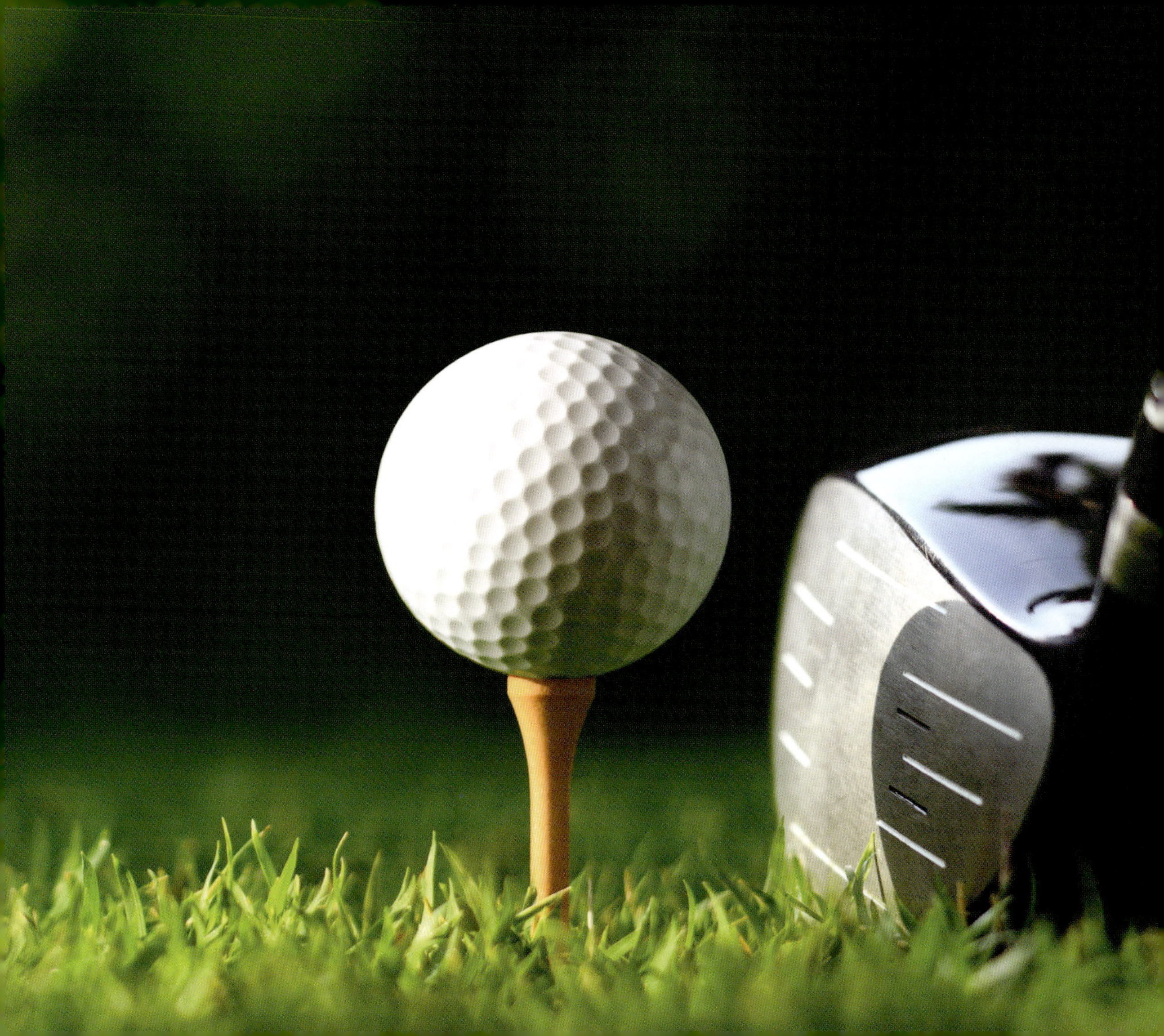

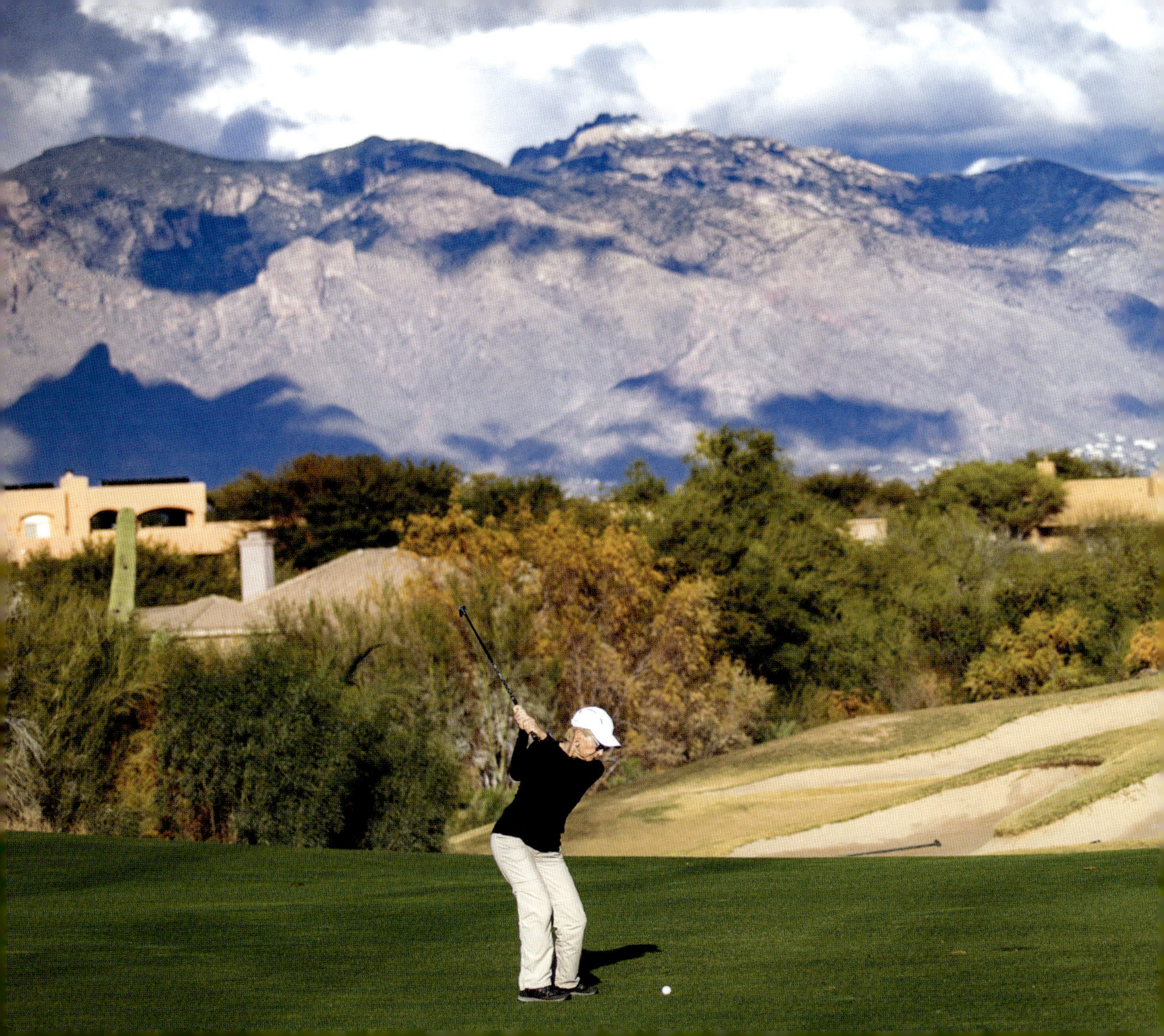

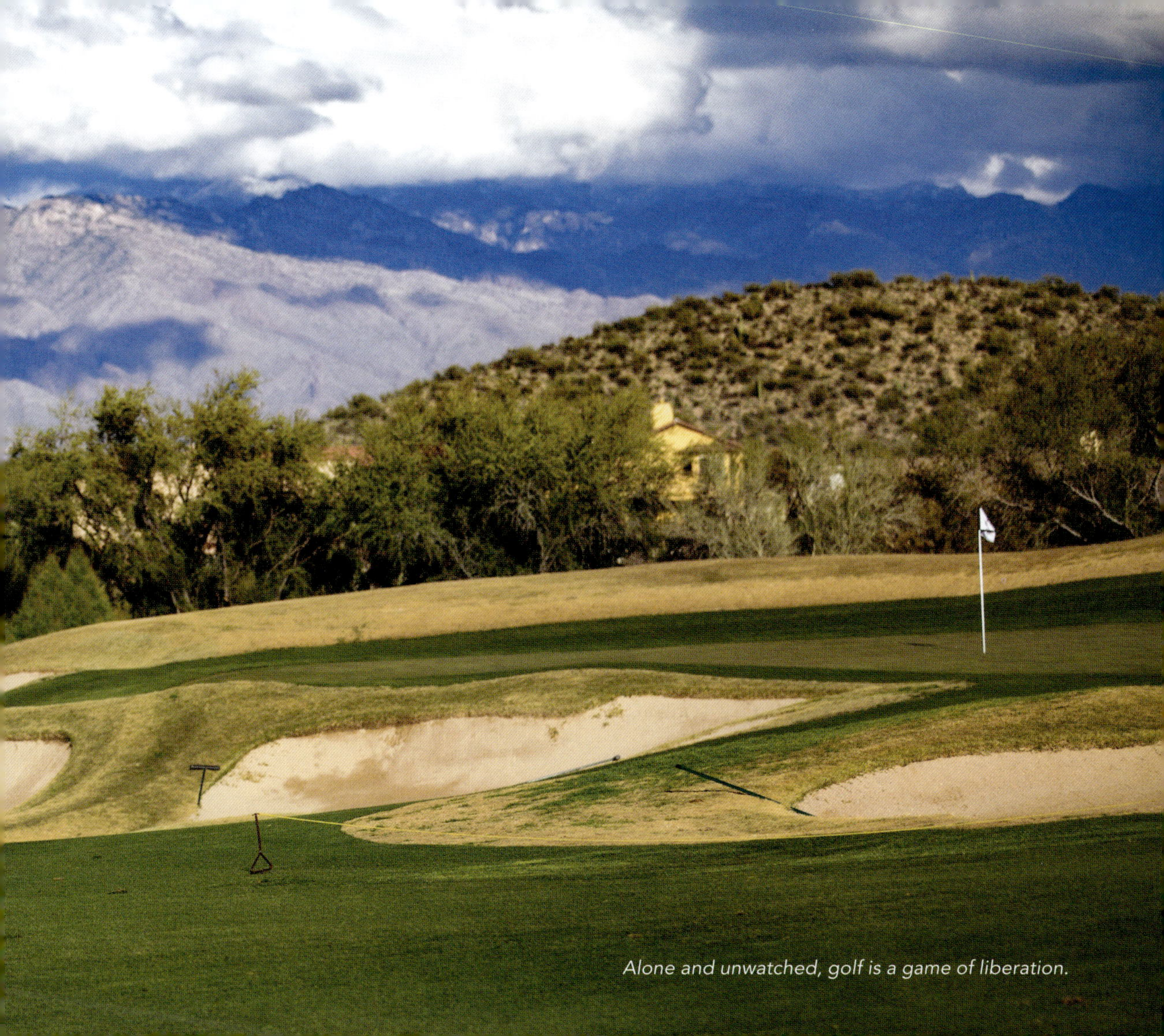

Alone and unwatched, golf is a game of liberation.

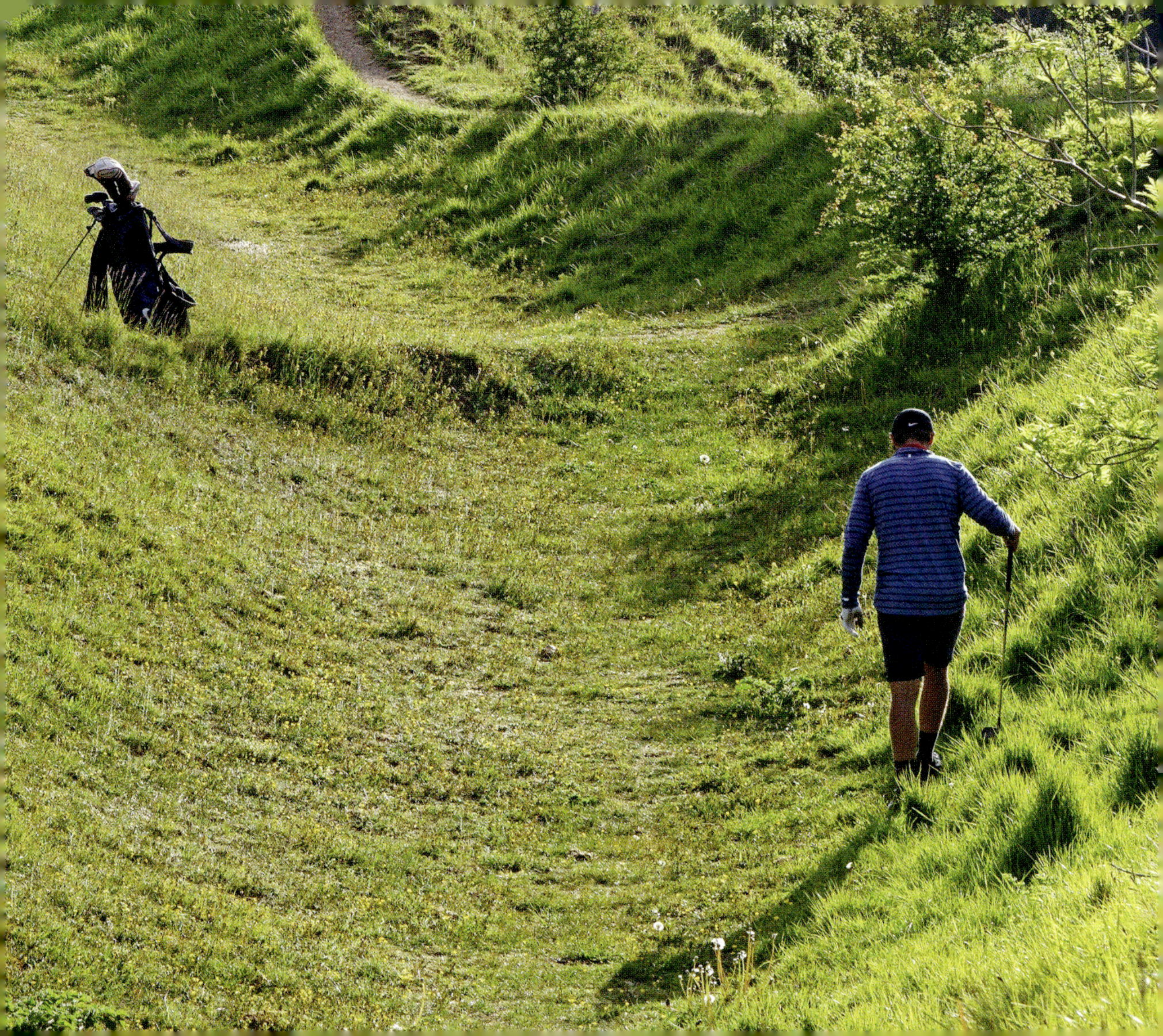

"Golf . . . is the infallible test. The man who can go into a patch of rough alone, with the knowledge that only God is watching him, and play his ball where it lies, is the man who will serve you faithfully and well."

—P. G. WODEHOUSE,
The Clicking of Cuthbert

WHAT IF:

Golf Courses Were Laboratories?

One of the greatest advantages of playing golf alone is the freedom it affords you to work on each facet of your game at your own pace and on actual holes (as opposed to driving ranges, practice putting greens, or simulators). Solo golf transforms a traditional round into a personal laboratory. It's not about perfecting every shot in a vacuum but about applying what you're learning in real conditions—under trees, in bunkers, on fairways, and across undulating greens.

From fine-tuning your driving to tweaking your short game, from perfecting your putting stroke to experimenting with your stance, from testing a new make of ball to trying out a borrowed hybrid, a solo round lets you devote your full attention to the areas of your game that need refinement.

And with no pressure to keep pace with others—indeed, you almost always want to slow your play when out alone—you have the luxury of time. Time to observe. Time to reflect. Time to try unconventional shots. A solo round is your chance to explore the game's possibilities without external judgment.

With that time, you can slow down your routine before each shot, increase the number of practice swings you take, or walk your lines before putts to familiarize yourself with green topography. That is, you can do whatever you like.

Similarly, without the judgmental eyes of playing partners or the pressure to conform to accepted manners and mores, you're free to explore new techniques, try out different strategies, and just generally push the boundaries of your game.

How would that look? Here are a few ways to treat the course as your laboratory:

LINE MAPPING: Use extra time to study green slopes and breaks from every angle, even if it's excessive for a regular round. Understanding how putts behave on greens can elevate your scoring consistency.

BALL TESTING: Try two or three different makes of ball over several holes, analyzing how they react to your game in terms of spin, distance, and feel.

LIE VARIATIONS: Hit multiple shots from different lies—fairway, rough, and bunker—to test how your swing adjusts to various conditions.

PACE EXPERIMENTATION: Play multiple shots with deliberate changes in tempo, swinging faster or more slowly than usual to understand how it impacts accuracy and distance.

APPROACH ANGLE TESTING: On a par-4 or par-5, intentionally place balls at different distances or angles for approach shots to simulate various scenarios you might face in a competitive round.

The beauty of what we might call the "golf lab approach" is not just in improving your skills but in discovering something deeper about your relationship to the game. It's a journey into your own potential—a way to explore not only what you're capable of but also how much joy you can extract from experimentation.

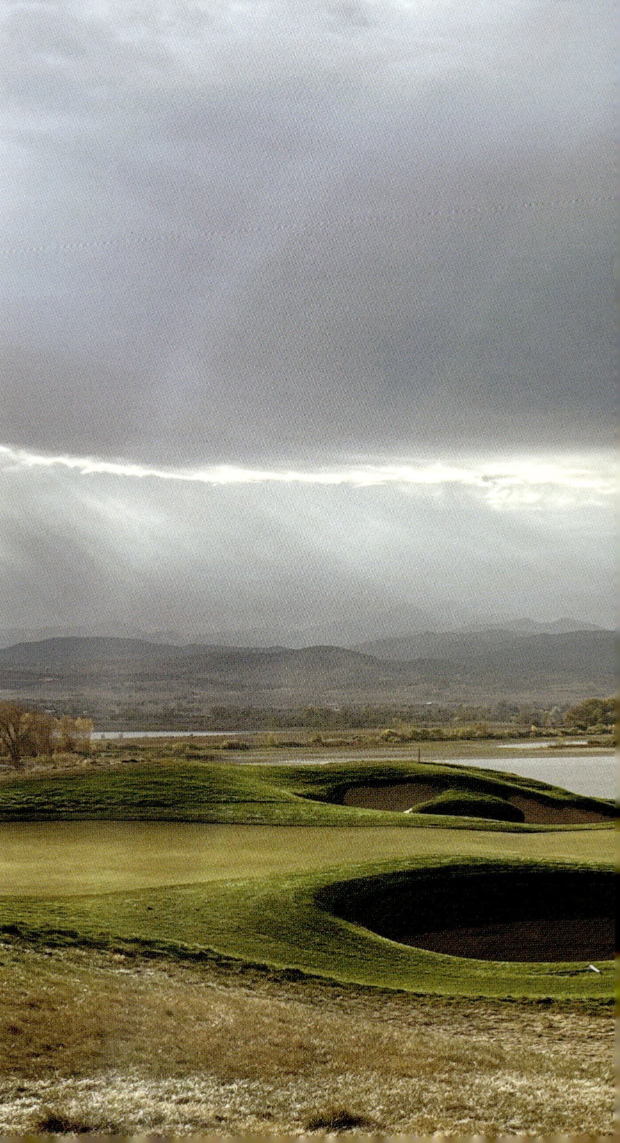

A solo round is best played in the liminal spaces of the golf world.

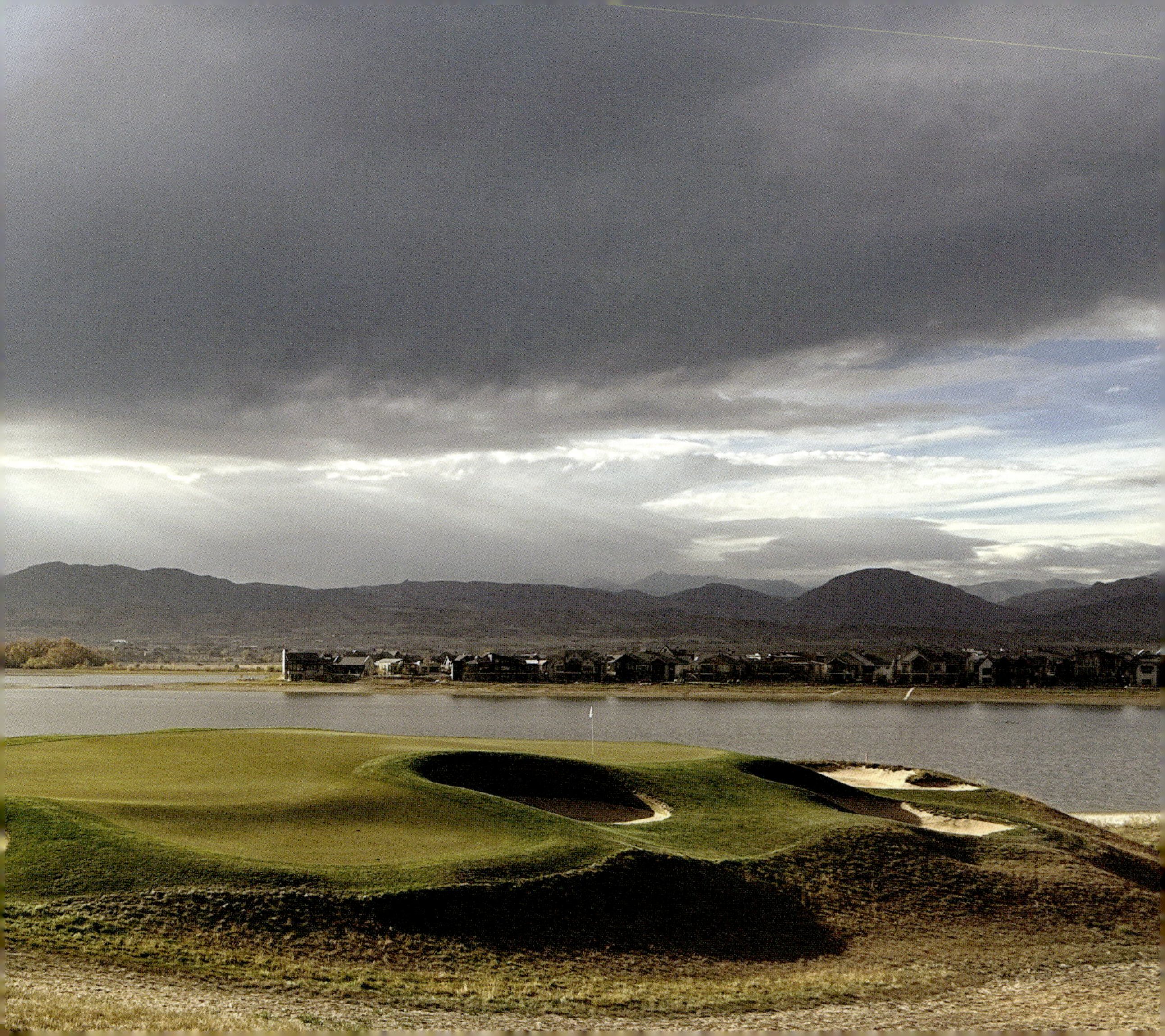

"The biggest thing
I learned from golf is embrace
making a mistake."

—PADRAIG HARRINGTON,

three-time major winner

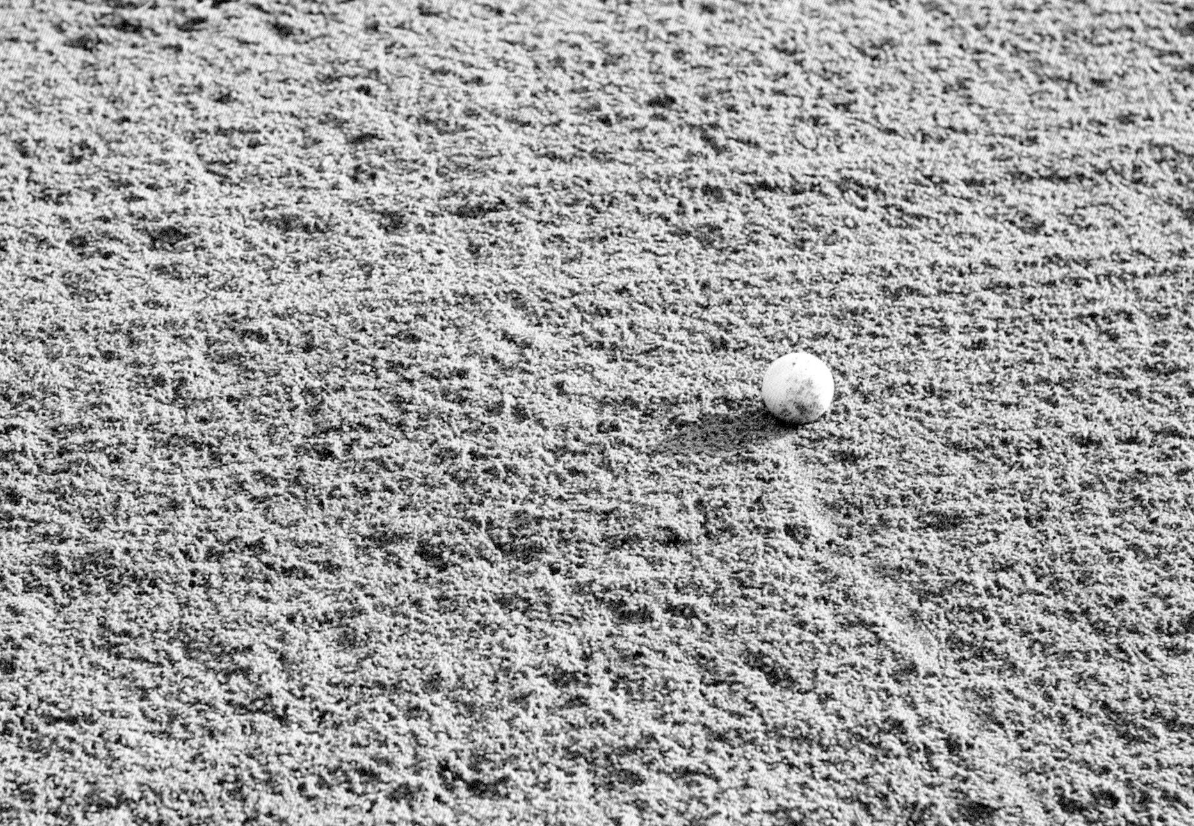

WHAT IF:

Golf Was About Invention?

Solo golf is the ideal setting in which to push your limits and make the sport your own. By inventing challenges and games, you can create a round that's both fun and educational. Below are ideas for drills and challenges to keep your solo rounds engaging and dynamic:

MULLIGAN BALL. The foundational experiment of solo golf: two tries at each shot using the same club, same distance, same approximate lie. If at first you don't succeed, try again. Mulligan Ball is also an opportunity to test two different makes of ball over a full round.

MULLIGAN BALL + WORST BALL. Same as above but always play the lesser of the shots. This exercise builds resilience and sharpens your course management skills.

ONE-CLUB CHALLENGE. Pick a single club (say, a 7-iron) to play an entire hole. It forces you to be creative and adaptive while teaching you a lot about your strengths and weaknesses.

TIME TRIAL GOLF. Set a time limit for each hole or for the round. This encourages faster play, tests your ability to make decisions under pressure, and improves your course management skills.

SHOT SHAPE CHALLENGE. Alternate between drawing and fading shots or manipulate your trajectory to navigate obstacles. This exercise is especially helpful for advanced players who want to master their shot-shaping repertoire.

ALTERNATE TEE CHALLENGE. Play each hole from a different set of tees, switching between forward, middle, and back boxes. This adds variety and teaches you to adjust to different course lengths and angles.

MULLIGAN BALL + HAZARD SEEKING. Take an old ball and aim it at hazards—lakes, woods, or out-of-bounds areas. Use your mulligan to recover from these situations, building confidence in your ability to handle trouble spots.

SCORECARD CHALLENGE. Create specific goals before each round—such as hitting a certain number of greens in regulation or avoiding penalty strokes—and track them on your scorecard. These alternative objectives shift your focus from traditional scoring and open up opportunities for unconventional strategies.

BUNKER BONANZA. Hit at least one ball out of a bunker on every hole, regardless of where your initial shot lands. Mastering bunker play is essential, and this drill ensures you get the practice you need.

ODD/EVEN CLUB ROUND. Play with only odd-numbered or even-numbered clubs for the entire round. This limitation forces you to adapt your shots and think creatively about how to approach different holes.

GREENS-ONLY GAME. Focus solely on getting your ball onto the green in as few strokes as possible. Once the ball is on the putting surface, pick it up and move to the next hole. This challenge emphasizes approach accuracy and shot placement.

ALTERNATE GRIP CHALLENGE. There are many ways to approach this, but a solo round is an ideal time to experiment with a wholly different grip than what you generally use. It pairs especially nicely with Mulligan Ball, allowing you compare and contrast throughout the round, but alternating grips from hole to hole is another way to go.

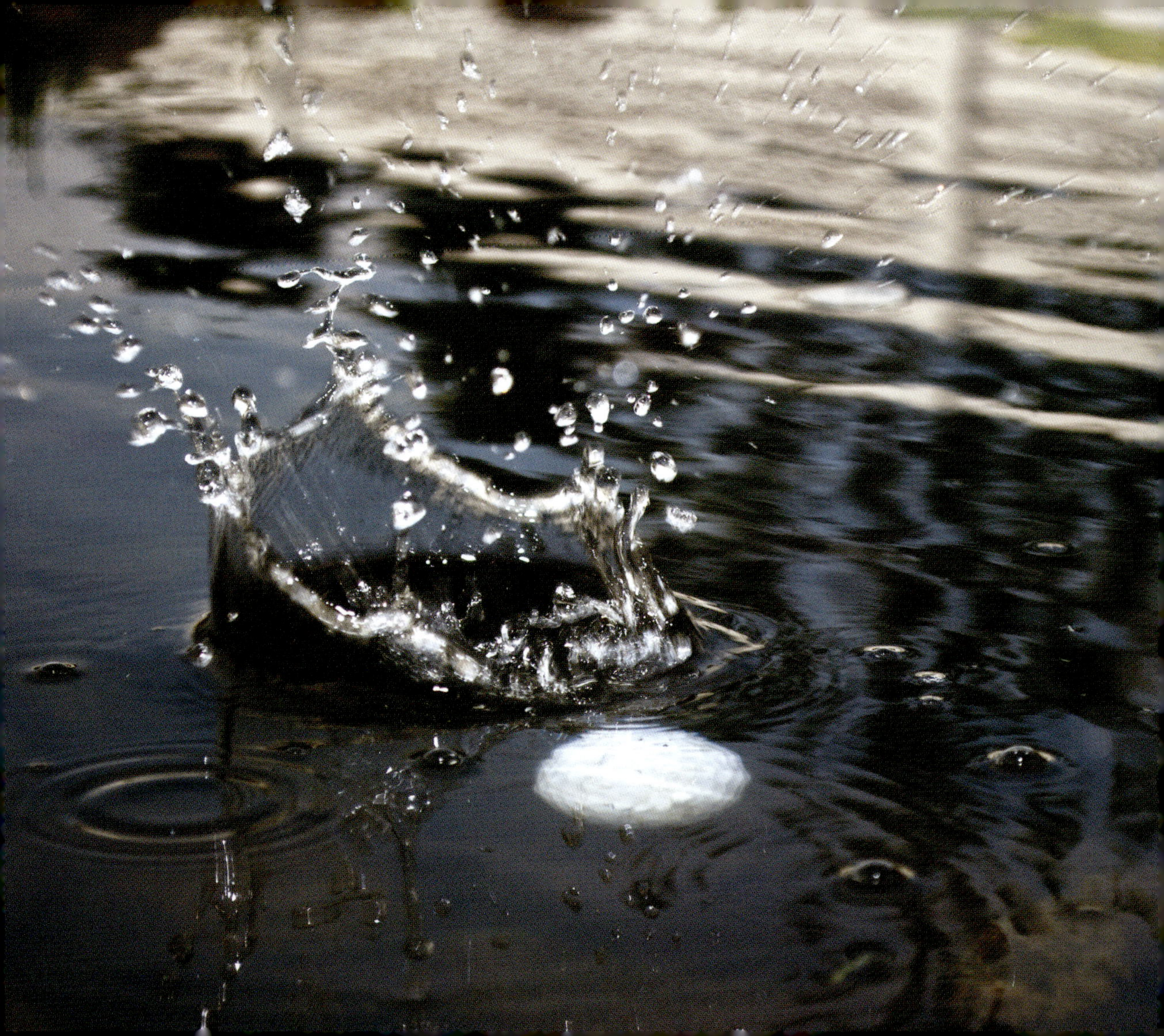

"Play happy."

—NANCY LOPEZ, *golf legend*

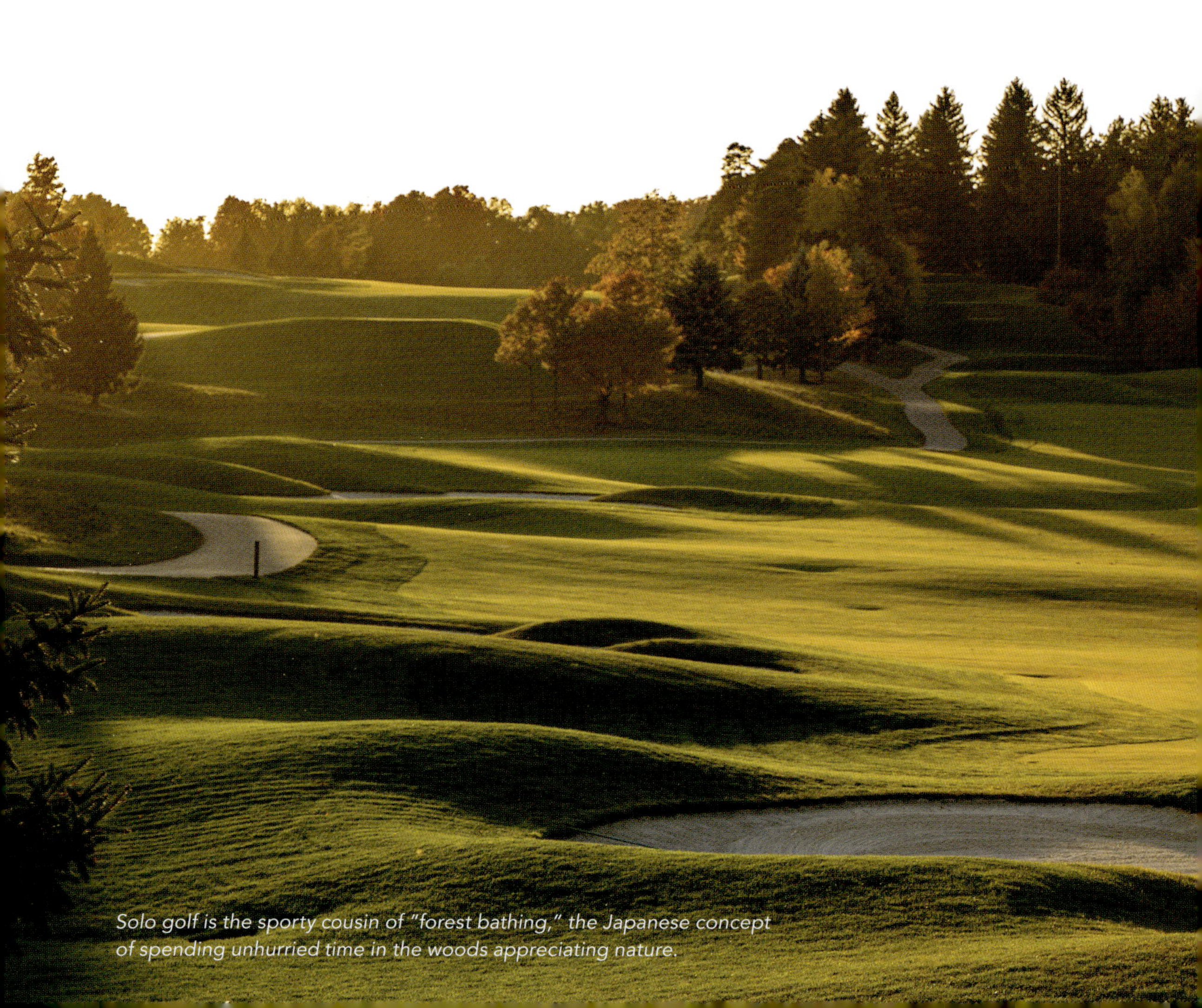

Solo golf is the sporty cousin of "forest bathing," the Japanese concept of spending unhurried time in the woods appreciating nature.

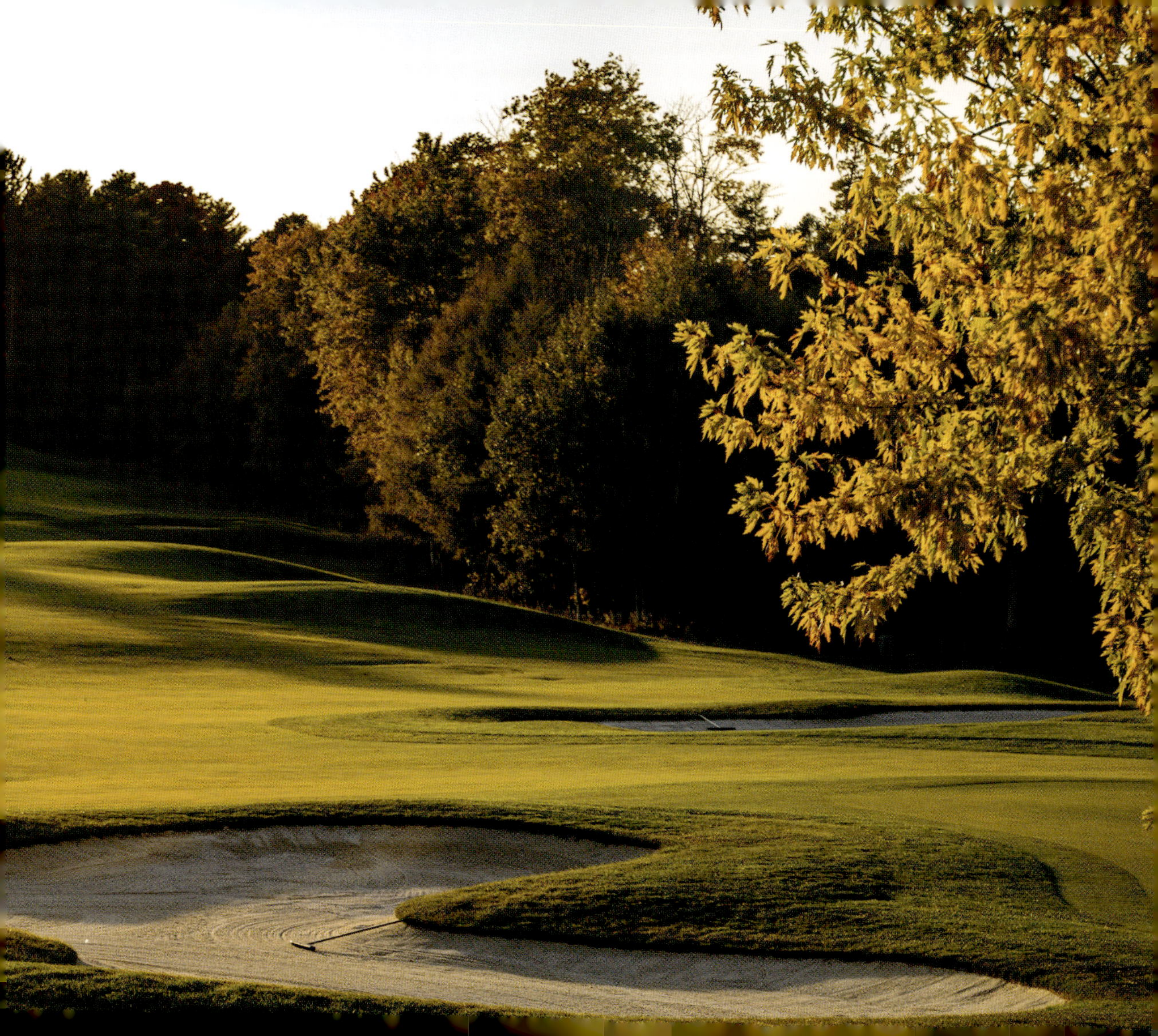

"Golf is the loneliest sport. You're completely alone with every conceivable opportunity to defeat yourself."

—HALE IRWIN,

professional golfer

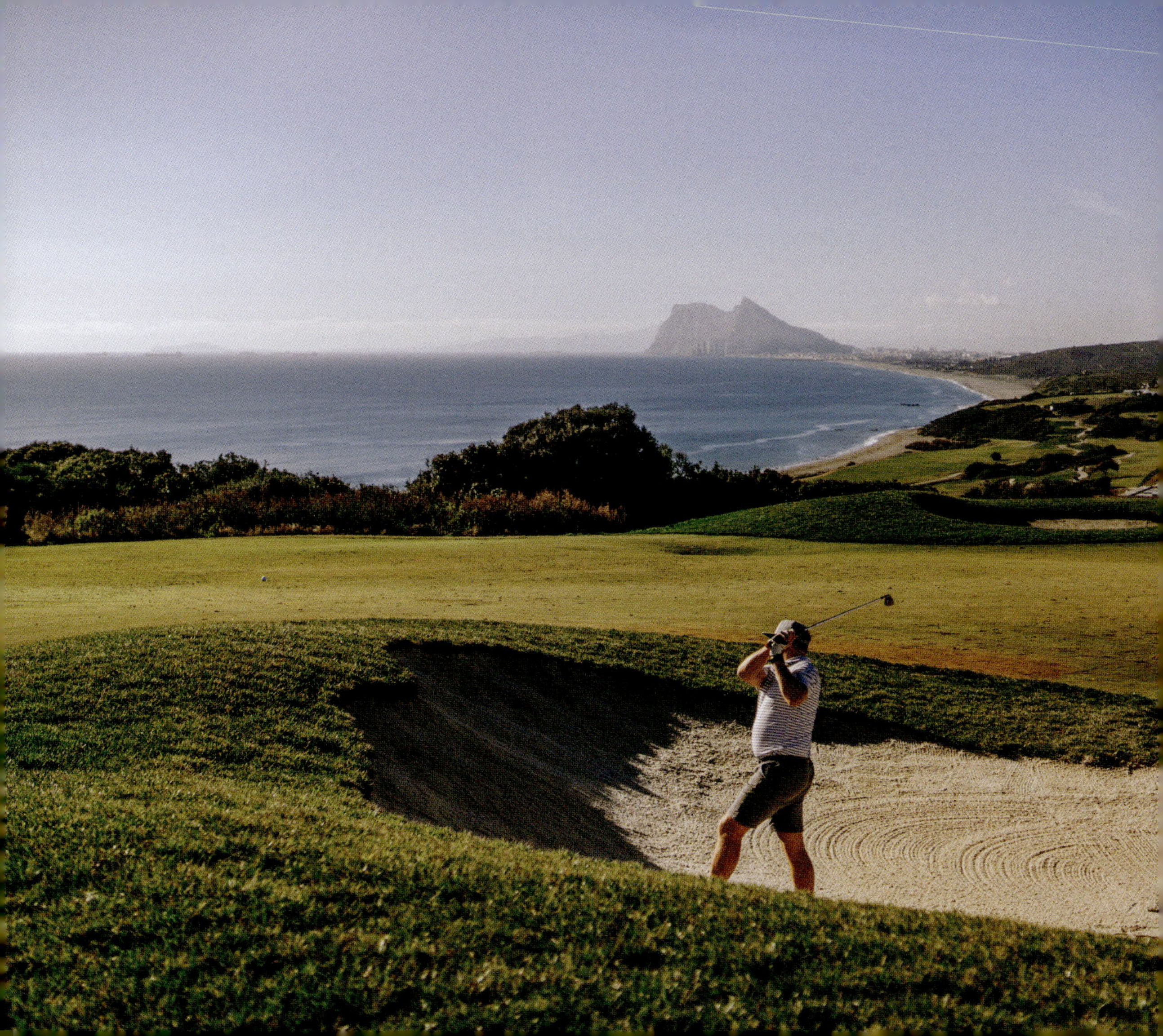

WHAT IF:

Golf Had No Rules at All?

Imagine a round of golf unbound by traditional rules, regulations, and conventions. What might that look like? What could it teach you? Solo golf offers the perfect opportunity to explore this boundary-pushing idea.

Here are some ways to play without rules and discover the game in new ways:

ARBITRARY RULE HOLE OR ROUND. Play a hole (or full round) with a self-imposed rule. Use only odd-numbered clubs, skip practice swings, or mandate a fade off the tee. These constraints encourage adaptability and can lead to surprising breakthroughs.

EXPERIMENTAL CLUBS. Play a hole using only unconventional clubs, like a putter off the tee or a hybrid for putting. It's a fun way to test your adaptability and creativity.

REVERSE GOLF. Play each hole backward, starting at the green and working your way to the tee. This unconventional approach forces you to rethink shot strategy and visualize the hole differently.

UNLIMITED MULLIGANS. Play an entire round where every shot can be replayed as many times as you want. Use this freedom to test different approaches and fine-tune your swing without worrying about the final score.

NO-SCORE GOLF. Ignore scoring entirely and focus solely on execution. Measure success by how well you hit certain shots or how creatively you recover from tough lies.

IMAGINARY OBSTACLES. Pretend certain areas of the course are out of bounds, even if they're not. This forces you to shape shots and plan routes with an added layer of difficulty.

"TARGET PRACTICE" ROUND. Assign yourself specific landing zones on each hole, such as aiming for a bunker to practice escapes or targeting a narrow section of fairway for added precision.

TWO-BALL STRATEGY. Hit two balls off every tee and play the one that lands in the worse position. This variation helps build resilience and decision-making under pressure.

The key with all of the above is to embrace the spirit of *play*. When you're not bound by traditional golf rules, etiquette, or expectations, the course becomes a canvas for your imagination. You can rediscover the pure joy of the game by focusing on exploration and self-expression rather than performance.

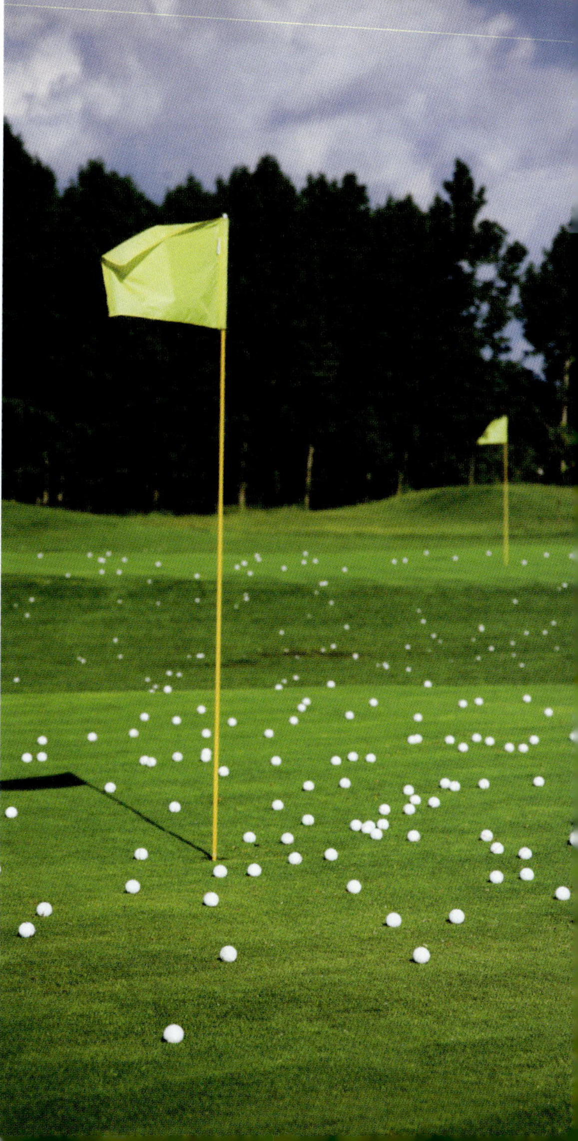

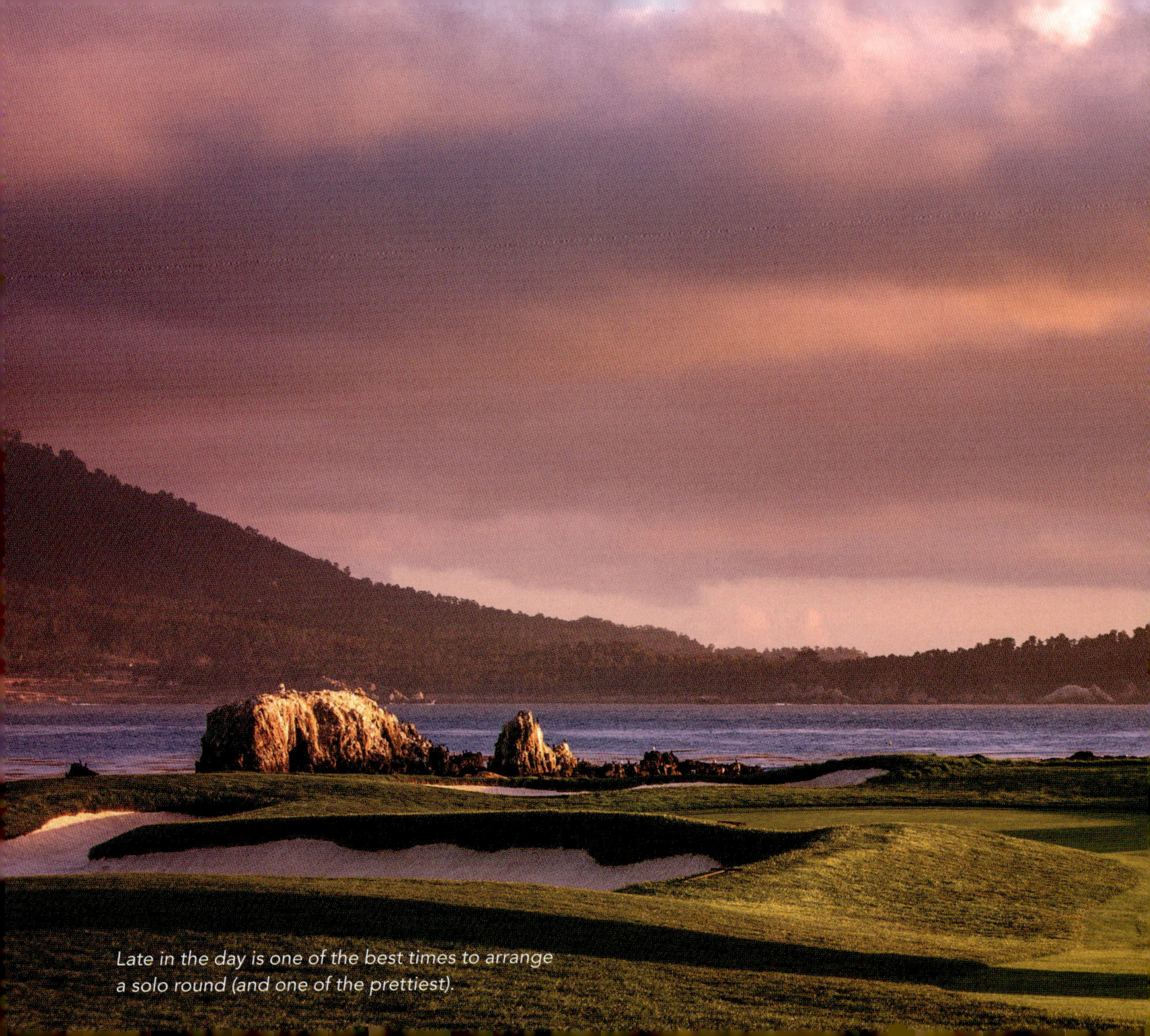

Late in the day is one of the best times to arrange a solo round (and one of the prettiest).

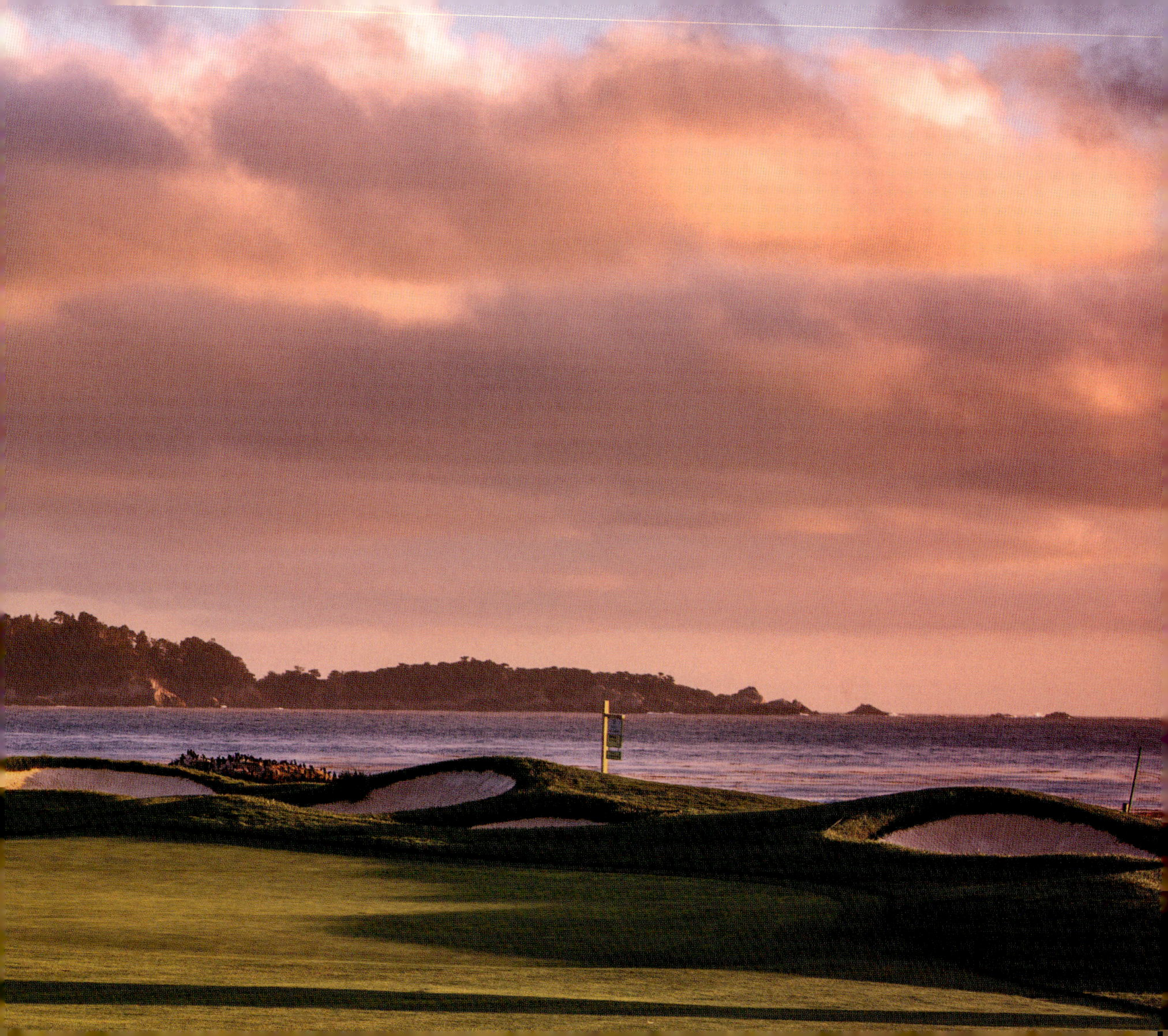

"The real joy of golf is in playing the game for its own sake, not for the score."

—HARVEY PENICK, *legendary golf teacher*

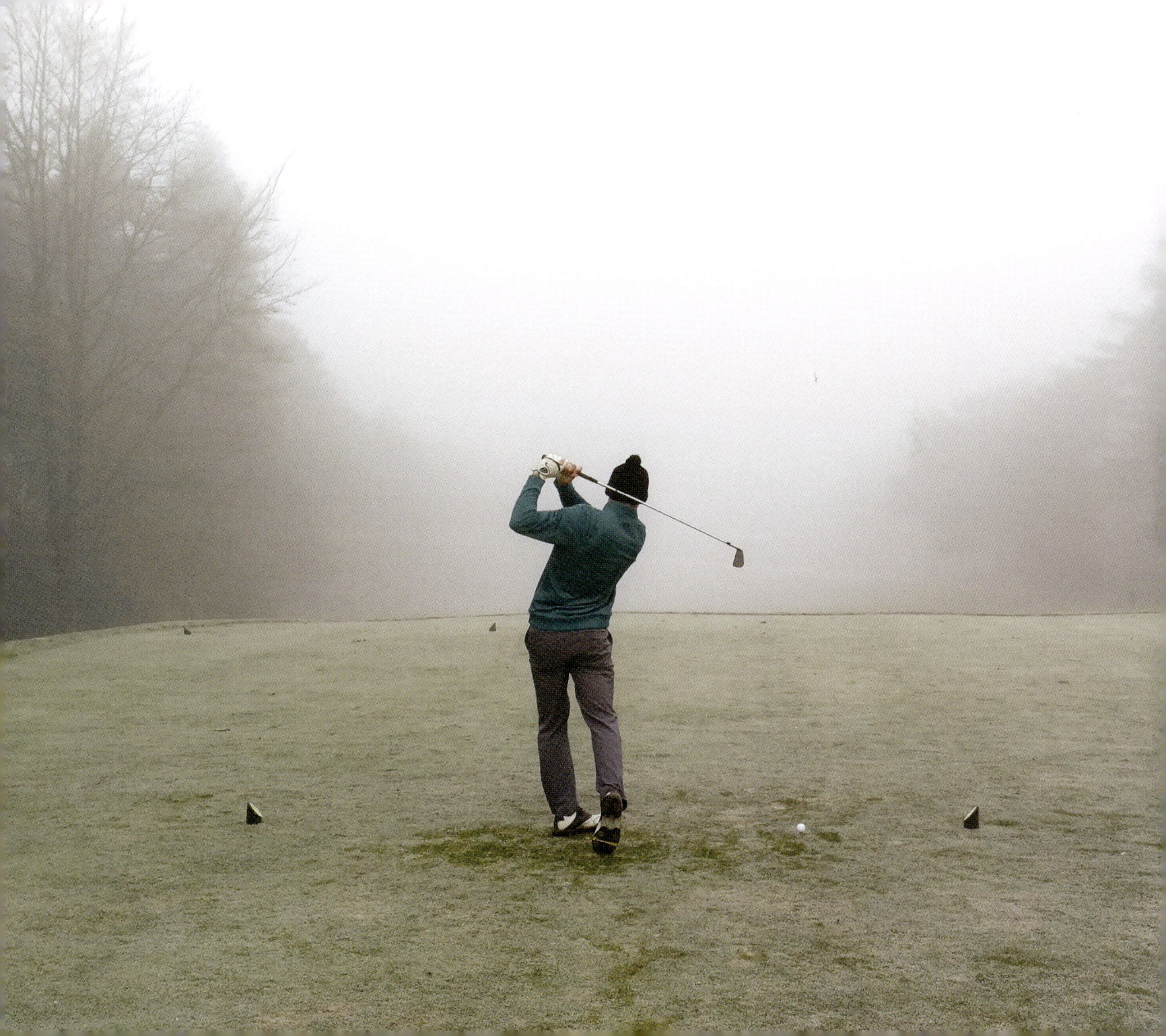

WHAT IF:

A Round of Golf Is However Many Holes You Decide?

If there's a theme in this book, it is liberation. More than anything, solo golf is a hall pass—from social obligations (of two-, three-, and foursomes), from rules (of play), from pressures (of competition), and, perhaps most unexpectedly, from the numerical parameters of an outing.

On many solo excursions, especially if you're playing late in the day, there just isn't time or daylight to play a full 18 holes, or even nine. For some golfers, this might feel like an incomplete experience. The notion of a "proper" round is so ingrained that playing fewer than 18—or even fewer than nine—can seem like a compromise.

But here's the thing: The idea of a standard 18-hole round is an arbitrary one, rooted more in history than necessity. Well into the 16th century, golfers in Scotland played on courses with as few as five holes, while some of their countrymen knocked around on courses with 10, 15, or 18. The birthplace of golf itself, St. Andrews, originally had 11 holes. Over time, the first four holes at the Grand Old Lady were deemed too easy and combined into two, creating a layout where players walked nine holes "out" and nine holes "in," leading to the now-familiar 18-hole structure.

Once you know this history, it's easier to reimagine what a round of golf can be. If the game's originators weren't bound to 18, why should you be? Solo golf offers the perfect opportunity to break free from this convention and redefine a round on your own terms—especially because your solo round cannot "count" in any way that matters to others, i.e., your handicap (see page 62).

On a time-pressed day, your solo round might consist of nine, six, or even just three holes. Or you could embrace total flexibility, playing four, seven, or 13—whatever fits your schedule, your mood, or the fading daylight. The freedom to adapt the game to your life can make solo golf not only more accessible but also more enjoyable.

This shift in mindset isn't just about convenience; it's about finding fulfillment in the game, regardless of its length. Shorter outings encourage focus and intention in every shot, helping you appreciate the experience rather than rushing to complete an arbitrary number of holes.

Think of the possibilities: Instead of hurrying through 18 with a sense of obligation, you can savor a perfectly timed six-hole stretch on a quiet evening. Or you might replay your favorite three holes, experimenting with different shots and strategies as the course empties out. By defining a round in terms of what works for you, you reclaim golf as a personal experience rather than a fixed formula.

This approach encourages a more intuitive connection with the game. You might decide to stop after seven holes, not because time demands it but instead because it feels like the right moment to call it a day. Or you might play an unconventional loop, skipping ahead or revisiting favorite holes, simply because the freedom is yours.

By letting go of rigid expectations, you open yourself to the true essence of the game—one that thrives on creativity, adaptability, and joy.

After all, in solo golf you're the only course official who matters.

One way to describe an empty golf course is "laboratory."

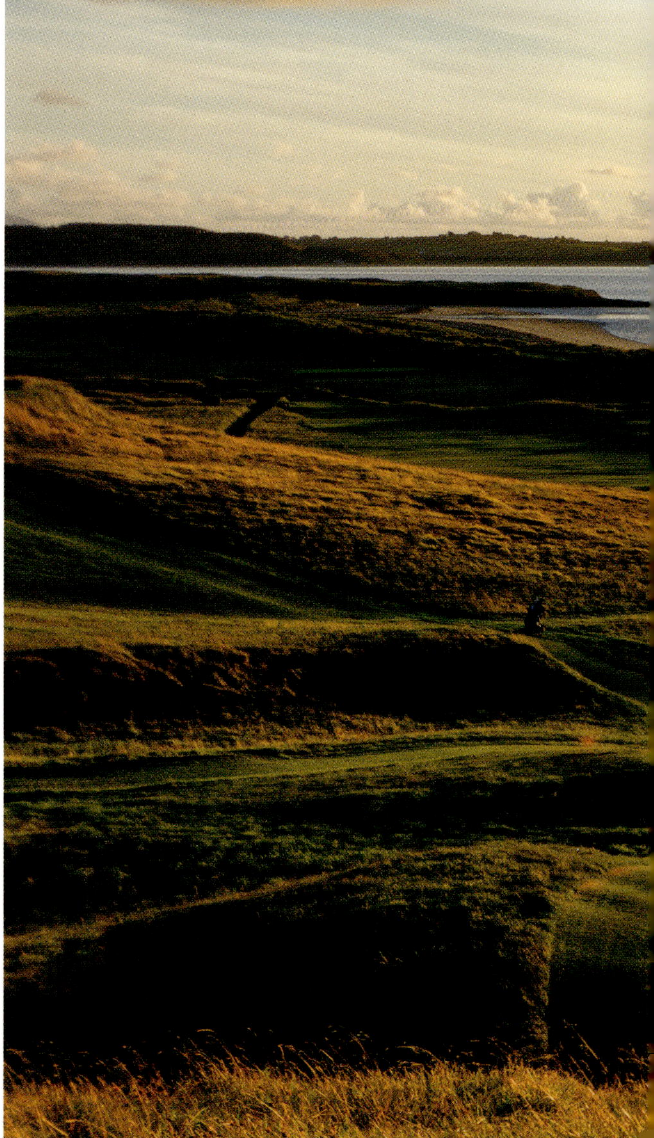

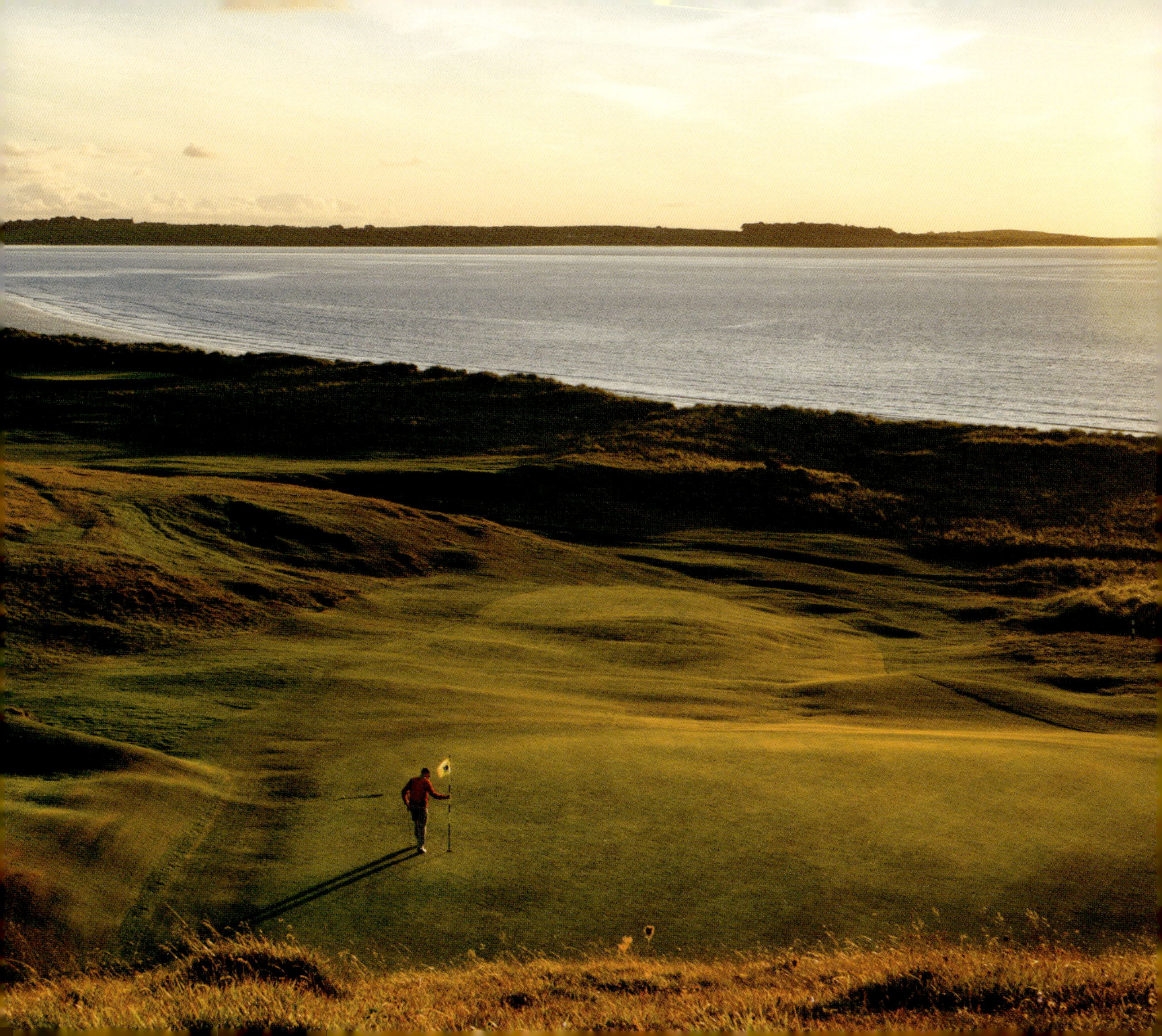

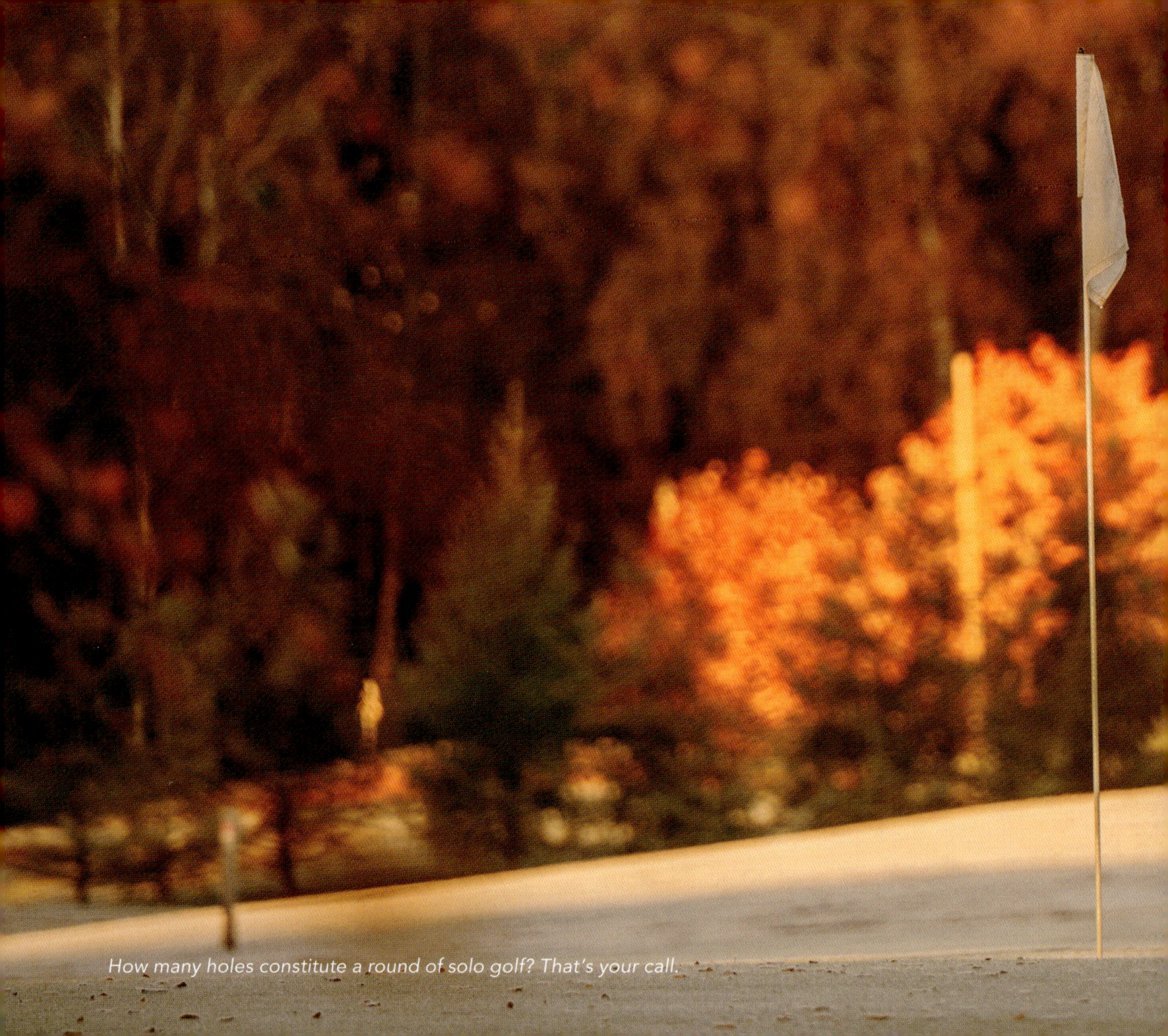
How many holes constitute a round of solo golf? That's your call.

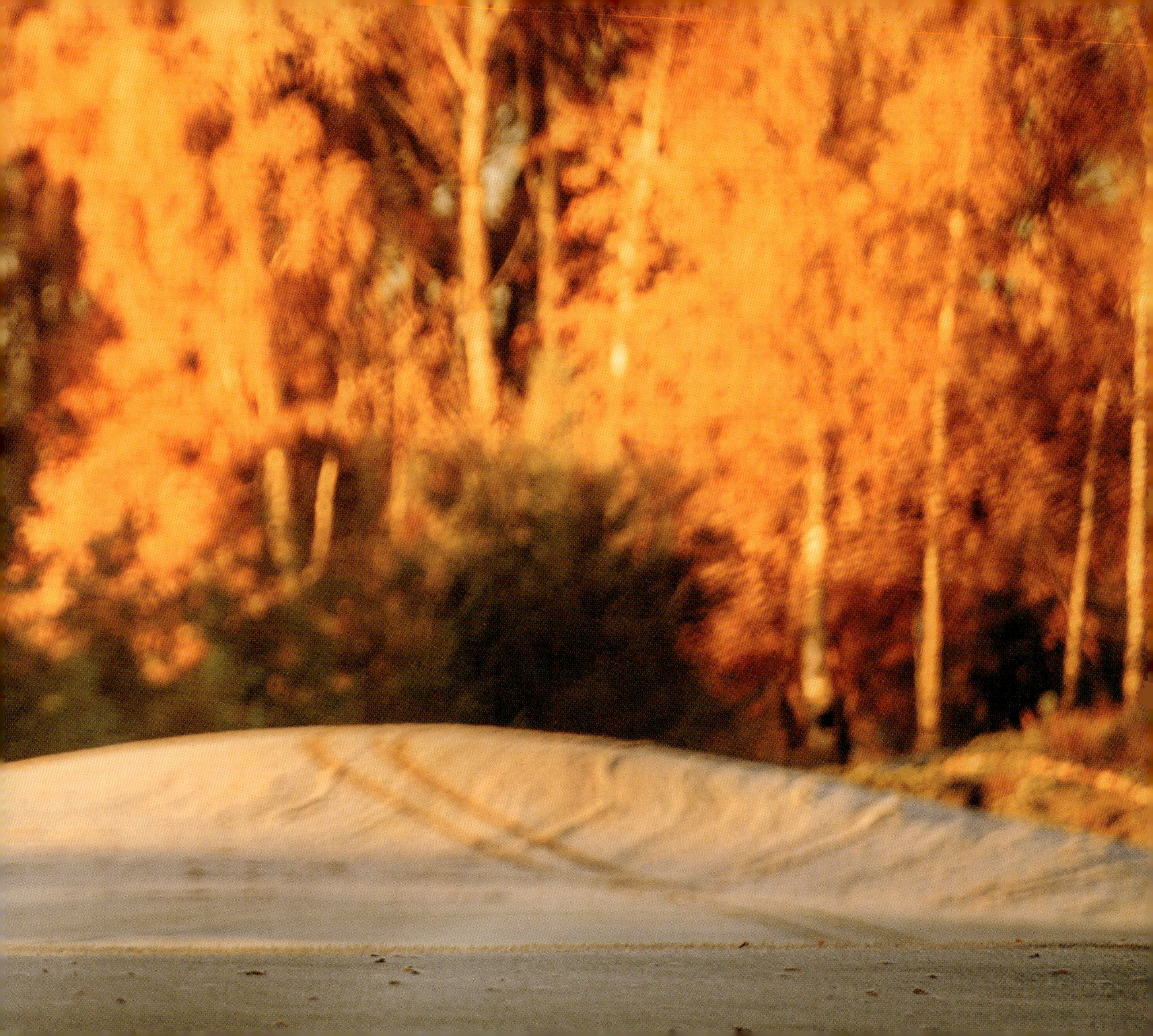

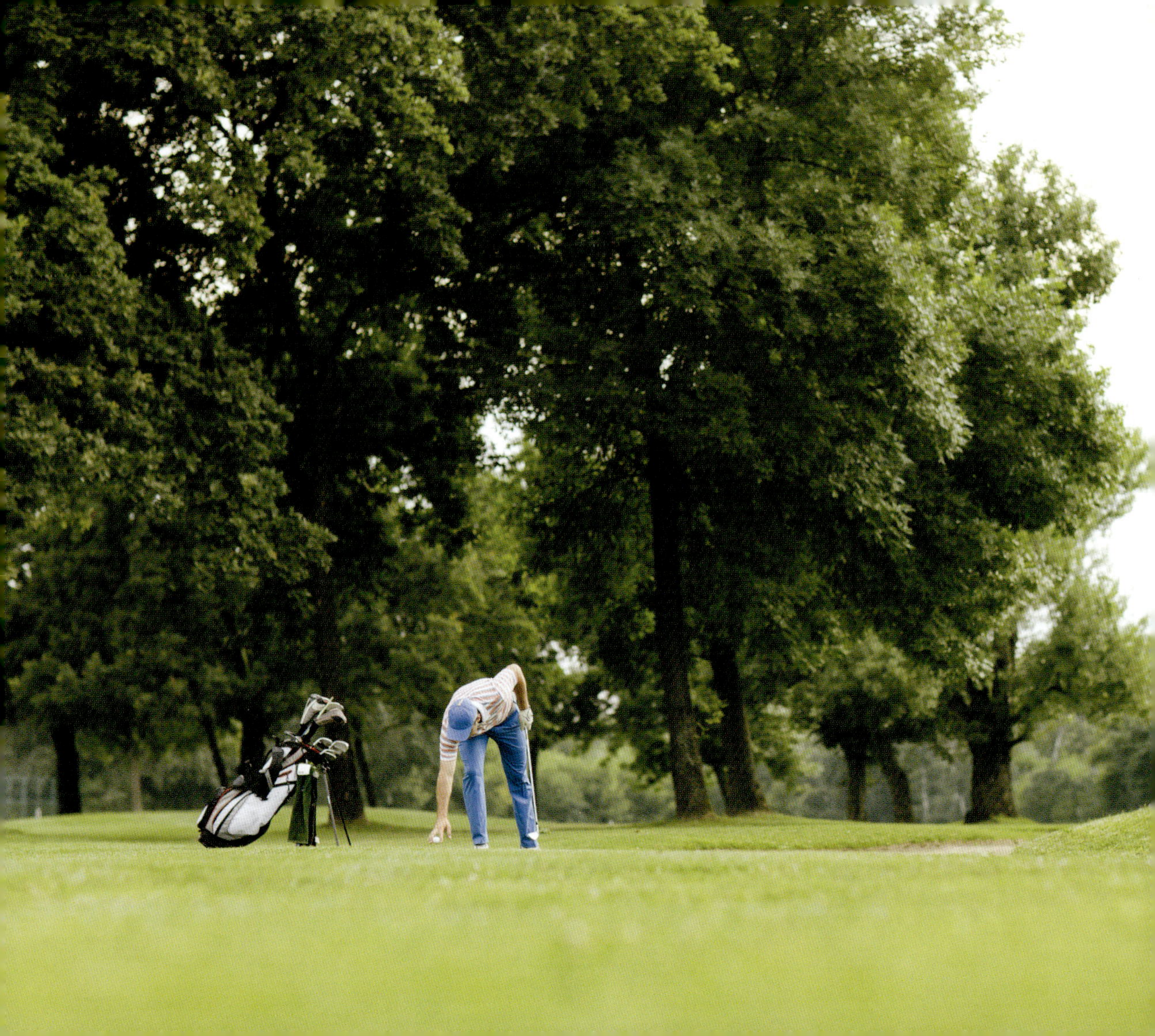

"The most important shot in golf is the next one."

—BEN HOGAN, *golf legend*

WHAT IF:

Golf Was a Race?

Golf's popularity as a recreational activity waxes and wanes, but enthusiasts of every skill and intensity level share a common complaint: The game is a time suck.

This is reality no matter where you play, with whom who you play, or the conditions in which you play. The most efficient twosome of scratch golfers on a private course playing in ideal weather will still require a minimum of four hours to complete an 18-hole circuit. Meanwhile, a foursome of high-handicappers on a crowded local muni track can expect their round to take five and a half hours, if they're lucky.

A solo round, on the other hand, can easily be finished in about three hours if the lone golfer in question doesn't have to wait behind any groups. And that's for 18 holes. A nine-hole round can, at some executive courses, be knocked out in about an hour, without even pushing it.

But what if you *did* push it? What if the goal wasn't just to finish efficiently but to finish as quickly as possible?

Of course, sometimes pushing it is more than half the fun. I refer specifically to "speed golf," a relatively new form of the game that is thought to have first originated in 1981 when competitive miler Steve Scott covered an 18-hole course in just under 30 minutes while managing to shoot a 95 (while using only a 4- and 5-iron).

Speed golf has, in the interim, developed into an organized competitive pursuit for aerobically minded duffers—Speedgolf USA hosts events across the country—but it's also an energizing change of pace for solo players, a radical but no less worthwhile departure from the typical golf experience.

The beauty of speed golf lies in its versatility. You can tweak the game to fit your preferences and fitness level: Jog between shots, walk briskly with a pull cart, or even use a riding cart for a modified version. You can choose to carry a full bag or limit yourself to a few clubs for maximum efficiency. The format can be adapted to you, making it an ideal way to break from the traditional pace while still sharpening your skills.

You can tweak the game as you see fit, but the biggest changeup is in the different mode of scoring. Basically, it's stroke golf plus time added, one stroke per minute. So, a round of 98 that's completed in one hour and three minutes clocks in as a 161. Over time, you improve your score by shooting more accurately or moving more quickly.

What makes speed golf particularly appealing is its ability to shift your focus. Instead of obsessing over the technical details of your swing, you're forced to think on your feet—literally. With less time to deliberate, your decisions become more instinctive, and paradoxically, your game often improves. Many players find that their swings become smoother and their choices more efficient when they're not overthinking every shot.

Pro tip: The best course of action for high-handicappers is clubbing down, exchanging distance for accuracy. When you're trying to hightail your way through a round, swinging a 7- or 5-iron often ends up being more of a time-saver than the rare flushed driver mixed in with lots of time-consuming hooks or slices. This approach not only speeds up your round but also helps build consistency and confidence with your mid-irons—skills that translate well back into traditional play.

If you're new to speed golf, start with a shorter course or limit yourself to nine holes to ease into the rhythm. You'll quickly discover how invigorating it is to combine the mental challenge of golf with the physical challenge of moving quickly. And don't worry about perfection; part of the fun is embracing the chaos of the faster pace.

Another benefit? Speed golf can be a perfect antidote to the tedium of a slow-paced traditional round. It reminds you that golf doesn't always have to be methodical and deliberate—it can also be dynamic and full of energy.

So, add a speed golf variation to your bag of options. It might well improve more of your game than just time spent.

There's a certain kind of beauty in speed golf.

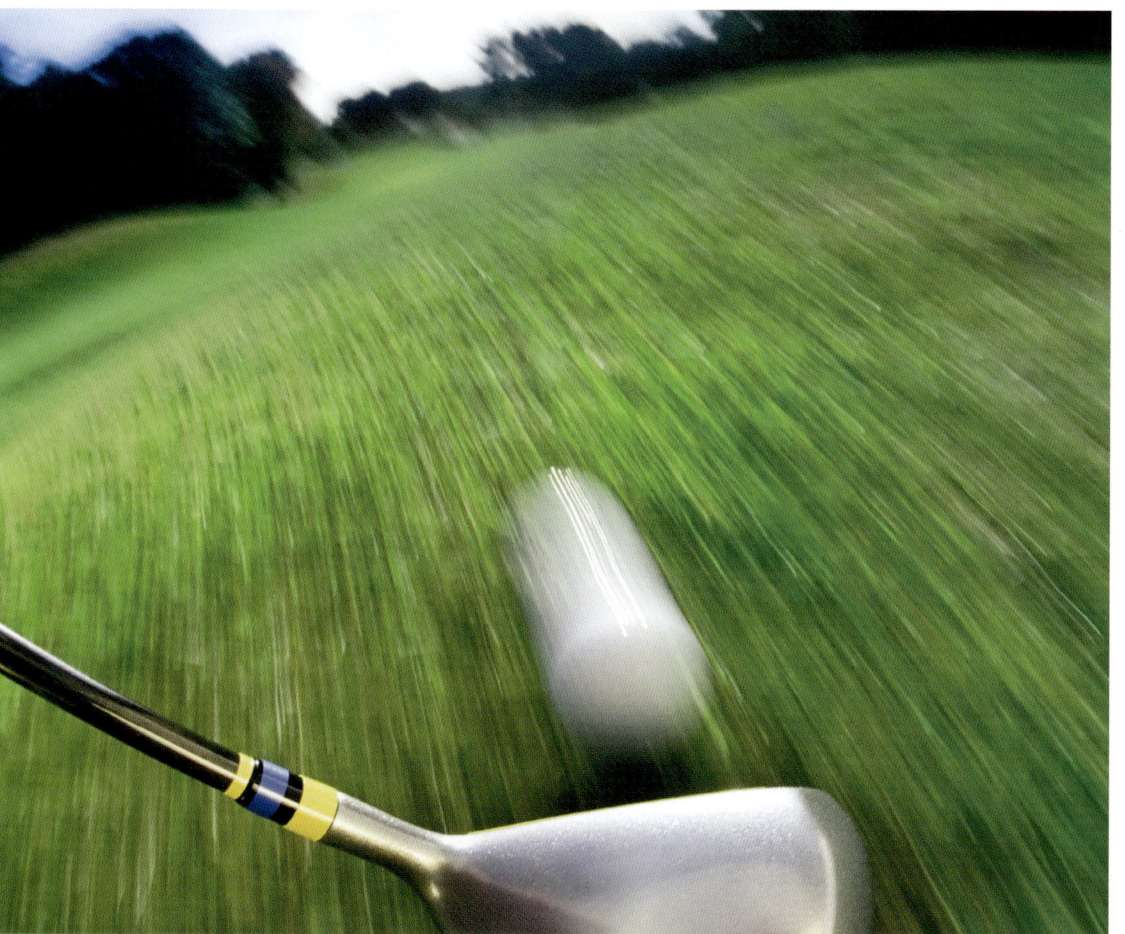

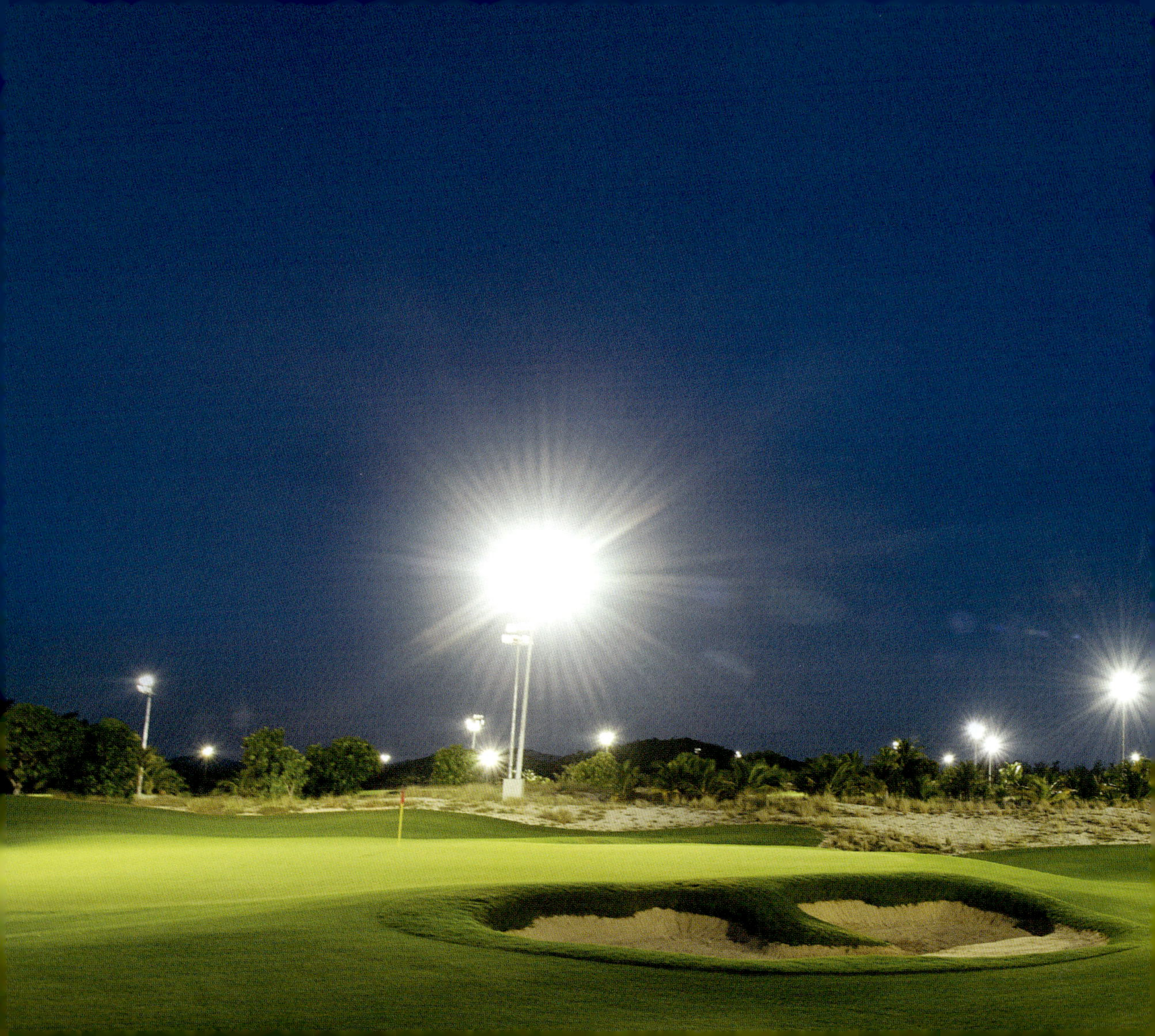

PART III

THE PRACTICAL

Solo golf doesn't just happen—it is a passion that must be pursued. This section offers the tools and tactics for carving out space to play alone, whether that means picking the right course, timing your arrival just so, or making your case to the gatekeepers with charm and grace. It's the behind-the-scenes work that makes everything else in this book possible.

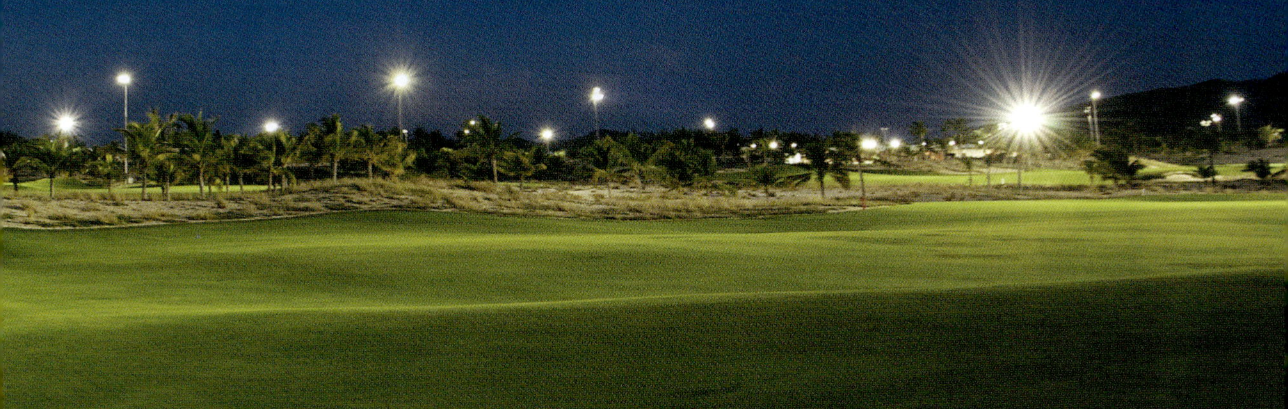

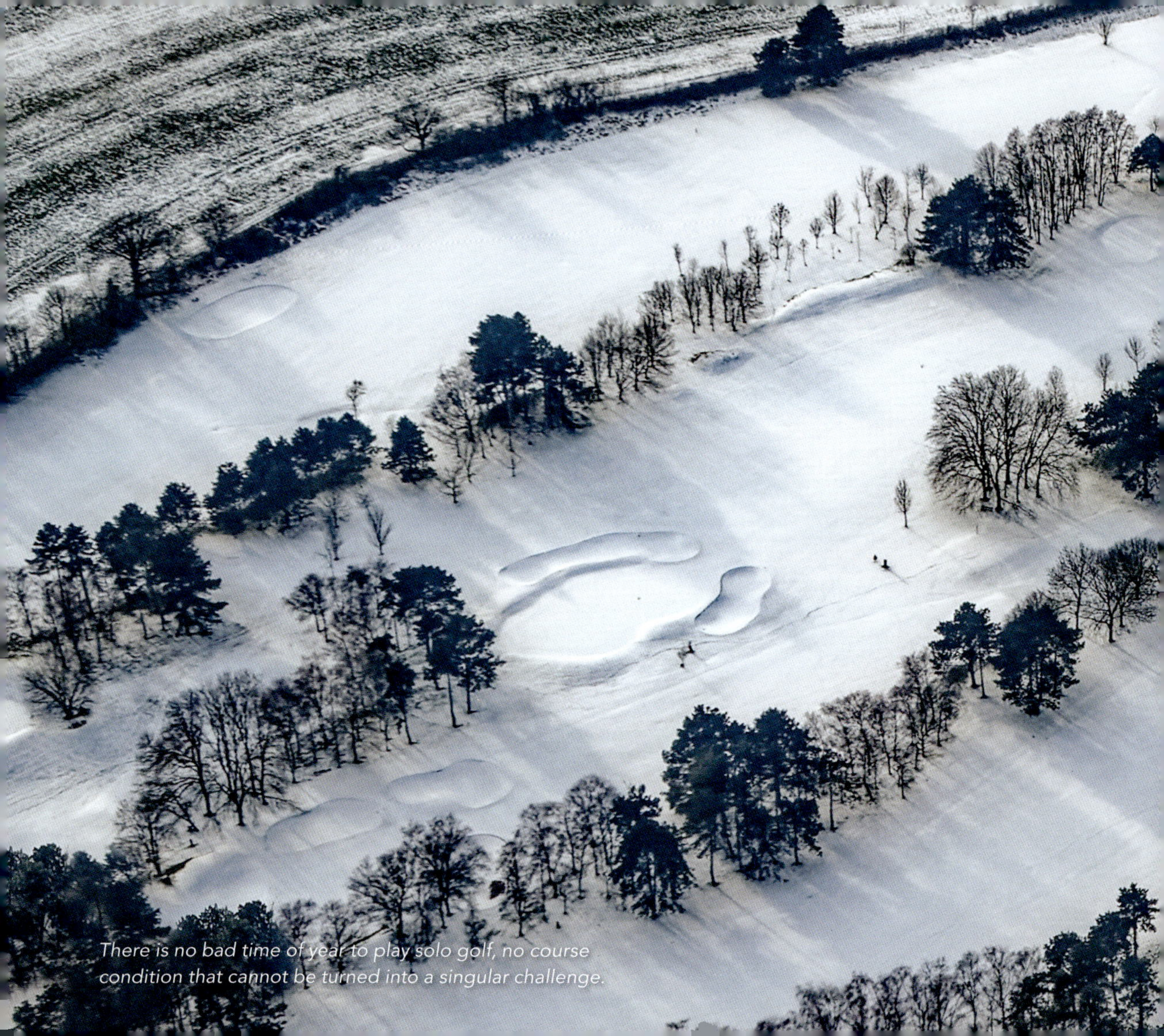

There is no bad time of year to play solo golf, no course condition that cannot be turned into a singular challenge.

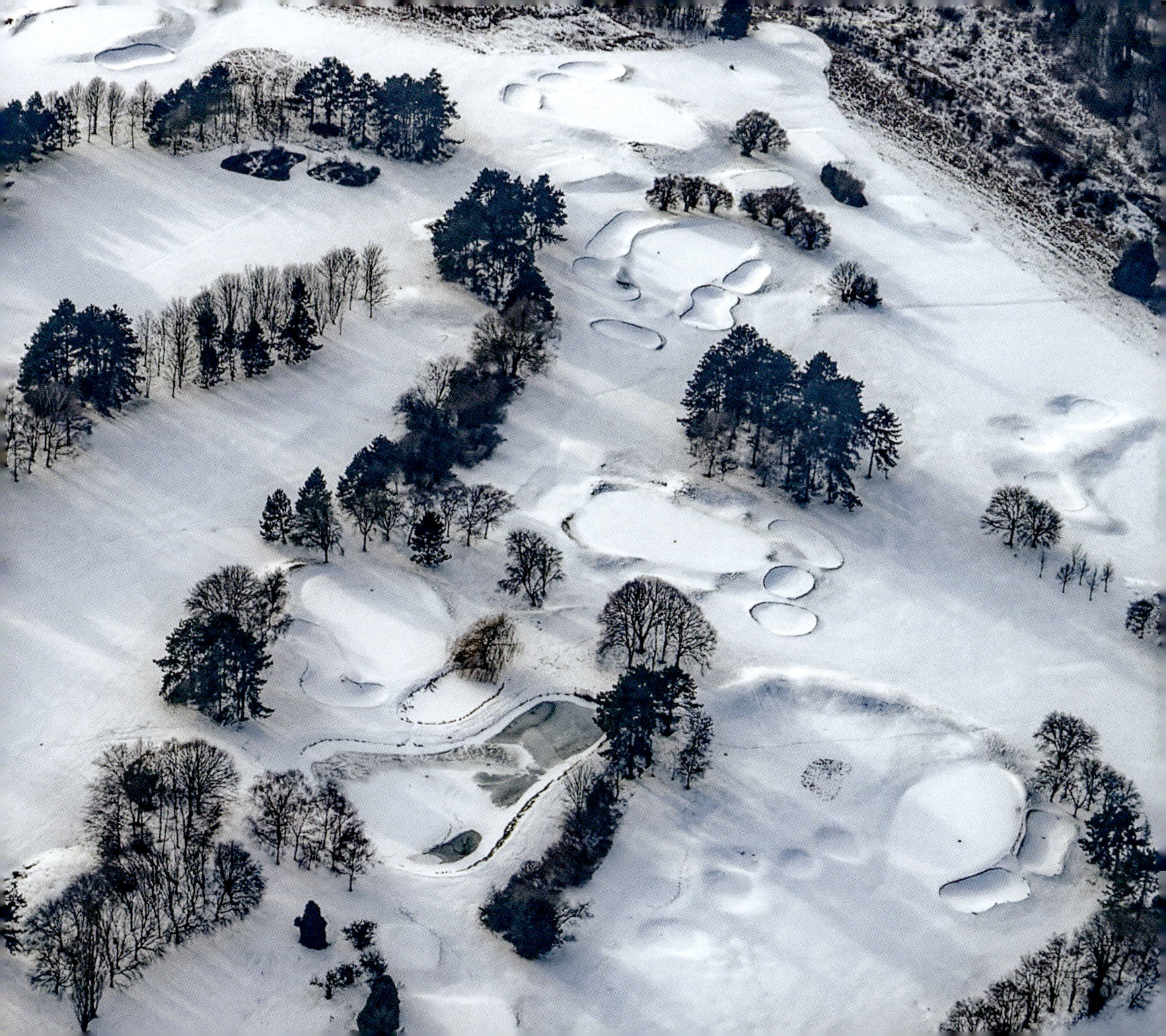

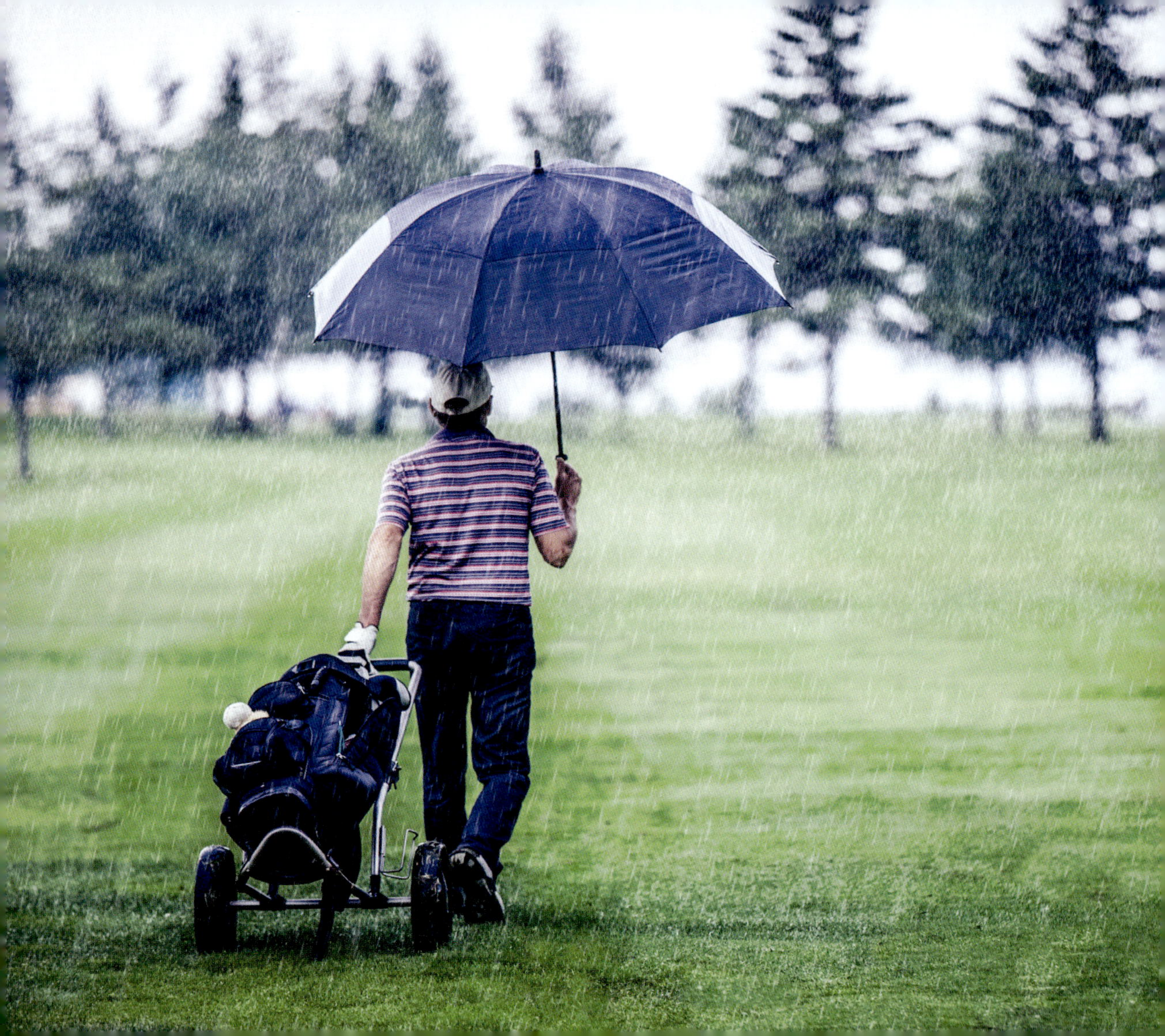

"The best time in the world for a solo round is with an umbrella in your hand."

—ROB ROXBOROUGH, *PGA Professional*

When to Golf Alone

Yes, finding a tee time for a solo round is very much achievable. But the overwhelming majority of golf courses don't make it easy to play by yourself, for three perfectly justifiable reasons:

DEMAND. Golf's popularity fluctuates, but these days about 25 million Americans play at least one round at one of the country's roughly 16,000 golf courses each year. (The global numbers are 70 million and 39,000, respectively.) It would be hard to get everyone on a course if starters had to do it one golfer at a time.

PACE OF PLAY. Most people prefer to go out in groups of two to four with people they know. All things being equal, on most public courses that results in a four-to-five-hour round, each grouping separated by 10 minutes, give or take. Nothing disrupts that rhythm more than a single golfer playing through.

MONEY. Be they public or private, fiscally healthy golf courses require lots of people who pay annual dues or green fees; the more the merrier. That leads to a decided bias toward allsomes over onesomes.

To be sure, you might occasionally luck into securing a solo tee time in the middle of the day during peak golf season. And though this might seem like a win, it often turns out to be a Pyrrhic victory. Having to repeatedly play through groups—asking strangers for permission to jump ahead, taking swings while they watch impatiently—can rob you of the peace and joy that solo golf promises.

Far better for everyone, then, is to pursue a round in the liminal spaces of the golf world—that is, those times of day, months of the year, and windows of weather when "normal" golfers are less likely to crowd courses.

Keep in mind, however, that a mindset recalibration will be in order. Generally, most rounds are planned, but the keys to golf in the shadows are adaptability and decisiveness. Adaptability, because sometimes you must be willing to hit the course at inconvenient hours and in less-than-ideal conditions. Decisiveness, because you have to be ready to grab your clubs and go, sometimes at a moment's notice.

Likewise, late fall and early spring can provide wonderful opportunities for solo golf, as long as you're willing to dress appropriately for cooler temperatures, occasional drizzle, and the odd dusting of snow. And winter can be an option in certain climates, too, especially on days when the weather unexpectedly clears.

Finally, don't underestimate the power of unpredictable weather. Many golfers will cancel plans at the first hint of rain or wind, leaving the course unexpectedly quiet. If you're willing to embrace a little uncertainty—perhaps keeping a rain jacket in your bag—you'll often find the conditions manageable and the experience rewarding. Some of the most memorable solo rounds happen under a light drizzle or with a brisk breeze, adding a touch of drama to the game.

For those prepared to play solo golf when the opportunity presents itself, the rewards will more than make up for any temporal or climatological inconveniences. You'll find the typical course vibe even more transformed during these quieter moments: calmer, more introspective, and uniquely yours. The solitude of these rounds doesn't just enhance your connection to the game; it deepens your appreciation for the entire experience of being on a course.

Your best chance of playing solo is when fewer golfers want to play at all.

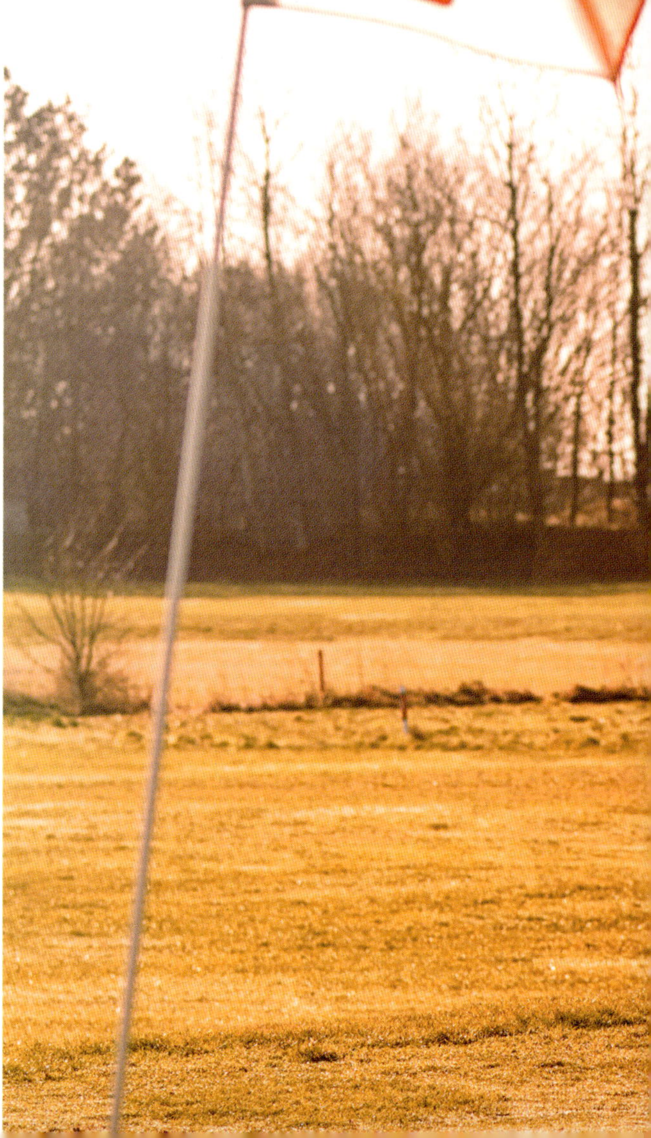

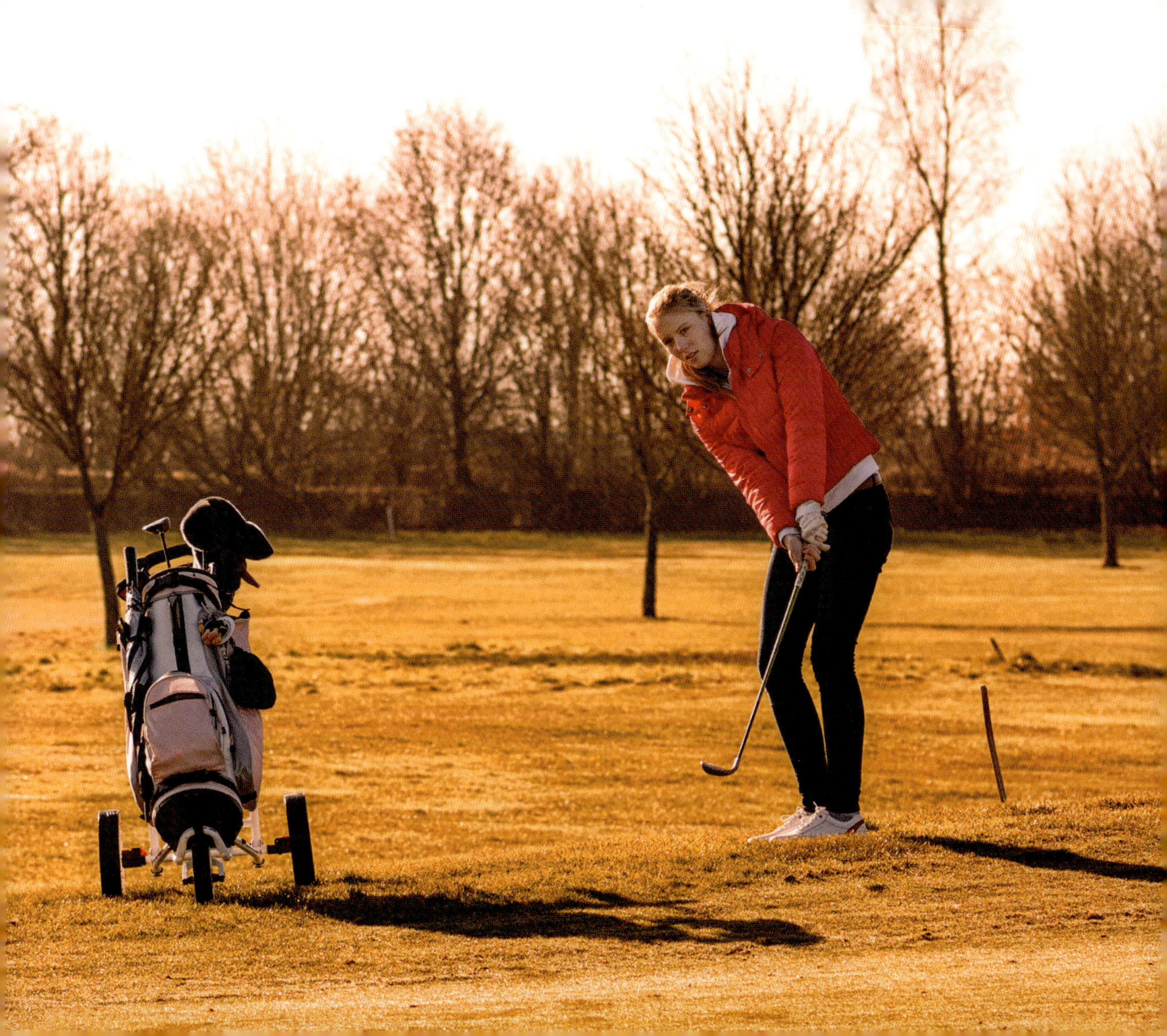

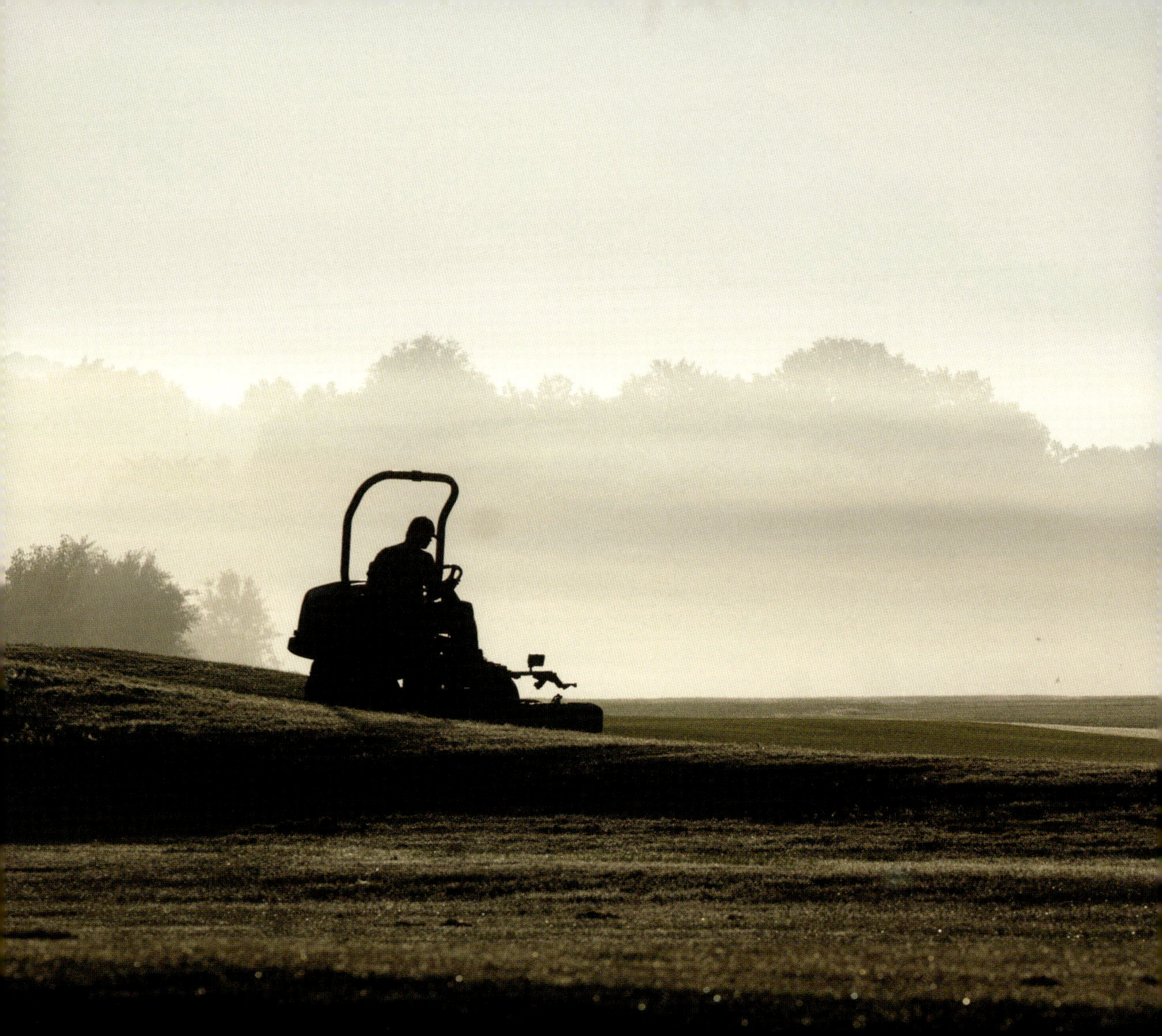

A SOLO GOLF TIMETABLE	
THE TIME	**THE TRICK**
WEEKDAYS	The majority of the roughly 500 million rounds played in the US annually occur on three days: Friday, Saturday, Sunday. The other four, then, represent your best shot at securing a solo tee time. That said, recent work-from-home trends mean more people are playing during the "workweek."
EARLY MORNING	Ideally, you should be "first out" (i.e., the first person to tee off). That leaves you to play as fast as the maintenance crew ahead of you allows. (And always be respectful of the maintenance crew.)
LATE AFTERNOON/ EARLY EVENING	If you're willing to risk rounds truncated by fading daylight—and you should be—many starters will be happy to set you up with a solo slot about 30 minutes after the final foursome of the day tees off. (Twilight rates are an added bonus, letting you play at a discount while enjoying the soft light of sunset.)
LATE FALL/ EARLY WINTER LATE WINTER/ EARLY SPRING	"Winter rules," colder weather, and end-of-season wear and tear to the course deter most golfers. But deterred golfers create openings for those more amenable to such indignities. Bonus: Expensive courses are often surprisingly empty during the offseason, a void that can work in your favor as you negotiate solo tee times.
INCLEMENT WEATHER	A dusting of snow in Pittsburgh, a light drizzle in Louisville, a July afternoon in Phoenix—bad golf weather is different throughout the country, but all of it represents a chance to snag a solo tee time.

"The ardent golfer would play Mount Everest if somebody put a flagstick on top."

—PETE DYE, *legendary course architect*

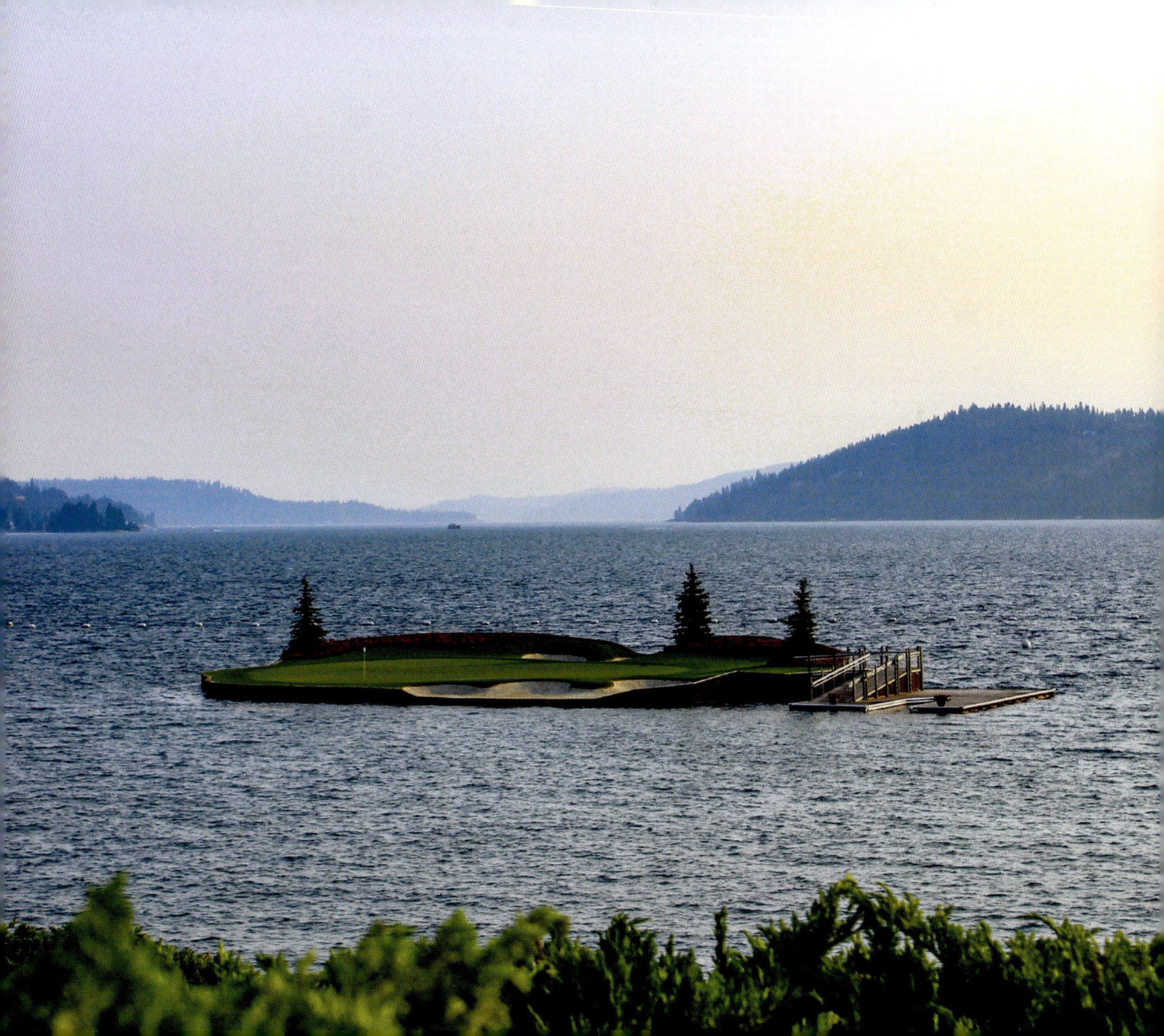

Where to Golf Alone

When I talk about playing solo, I sometimes describe it as "bootleg golf" or "grunge golf" or "scrappy golf"—that is, a rawer, realer version of the typical outing. It's this unfiltered experience that strips away some of the polish and replaces it with something more authentic.

Half of the spirit I'm trying to convey arises from the time of day one plays or the weather one plays in (see page 117). But the other half is a function of *where* you play, that is, the kinds of courses you frequent.

Although I have played alone at some beautifully designed, well-tended clubs, the majority of my solo rounds have been spent at what some might call grinder tracks: municipal courses (both in the United States and other countries) that are unlikely to host even a bachelor party outing, let alone a tournament for an organized golf tour.

There's a grittiness to such courses, even the relatively well-maintained ones—a janky quality that in many ways harkens back to golf's earliest origins, when courses emerged from natural topographical features and wildlife sheltering patterns. The quirks become part of their charm: crusty tee box divots, weedy fairways, scruffy second cuts, pebbly sand traps, and splotchy greens. Playing solo on these tracks feels like a journey back in time.

Now you're in third-century Europe, when Roman soldiers swatted feather-stuffed balls across open fields in the downtime between sieging and sacking.

Now you're in 12th-century Netherlands, when "sportsmen" occupied their free hours by seeing who could whack grass-stuffed leather balls the farthest over open pastures.

Now you're back in 13th-century Scotland, with those lonesome shepherds and their petrified sheep dung.

And now you're in 14th-century China, where members of the royal court used long sticks to knock little balls into little holes marked with flags, according to one surviving drawing from the Ming dynasty.

This historical tapestry adds a richness to your solo rounds, a reminder that golf's origins were as humble and inventive as the courses you now find yourself exploring. Even the grittiest municipal track carries echoes of those early experiments with ball and stick.

Playing on such courses also challenges you to adopt a different mindset. Every hardpan lie or concretized divot is not the bad luck it might feel like in a high-stakes group round. Instead, it's a test of your ingenuity, a chance to "use the difficulty," as actor Michael Caine famously described the art of finding benefit in life's small hiccups, medium predicaments, and major setbacks.

On these courses, every obstacle becomes an opportunity. That bare patch of grass forces you to focus on precision. That scruffy bunker tests your creativity with shot-making from a hazard. Each challenge is a chance to MacGyver your way out of trouble and into the hole, turning what might otherwise feel like

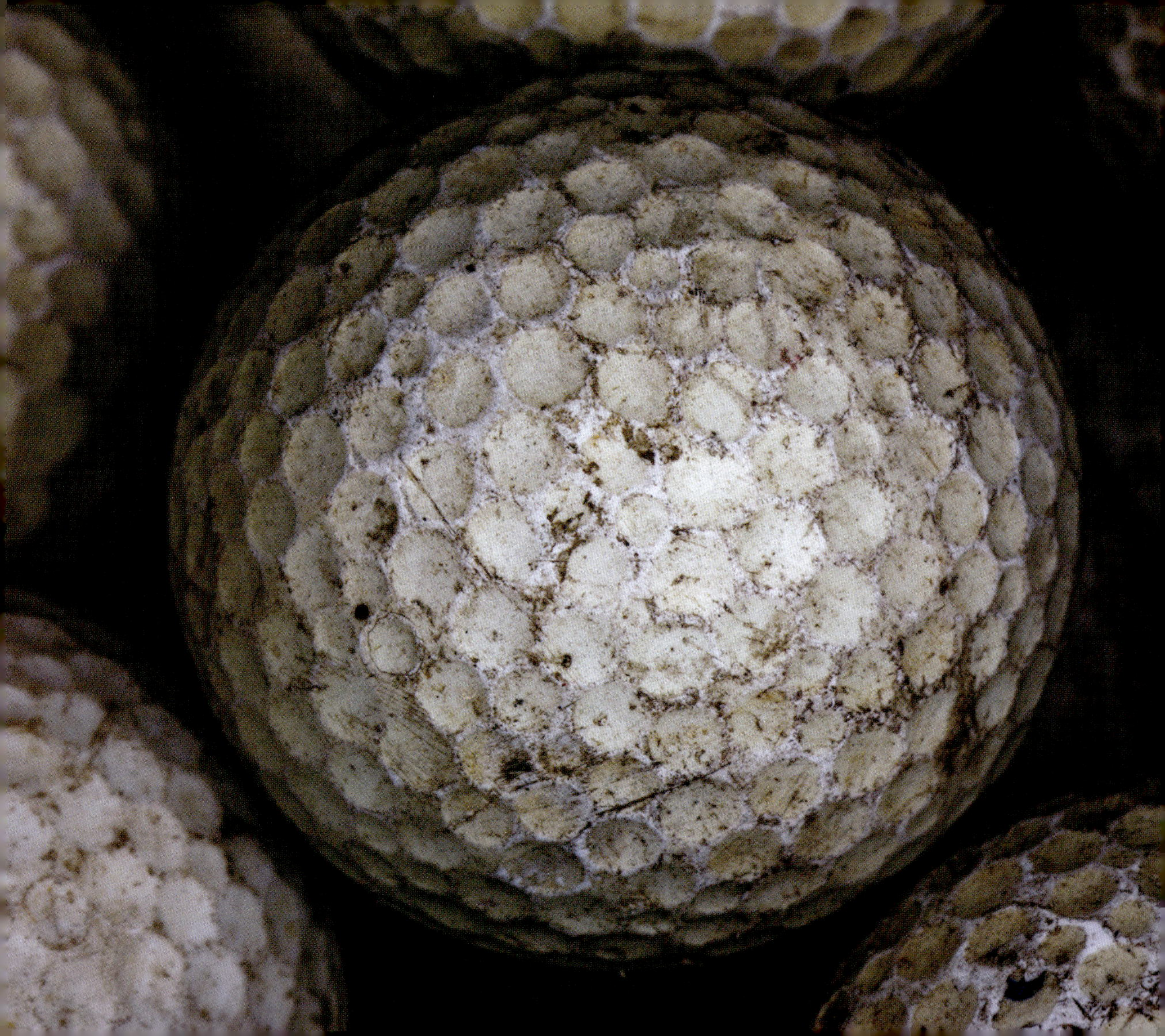

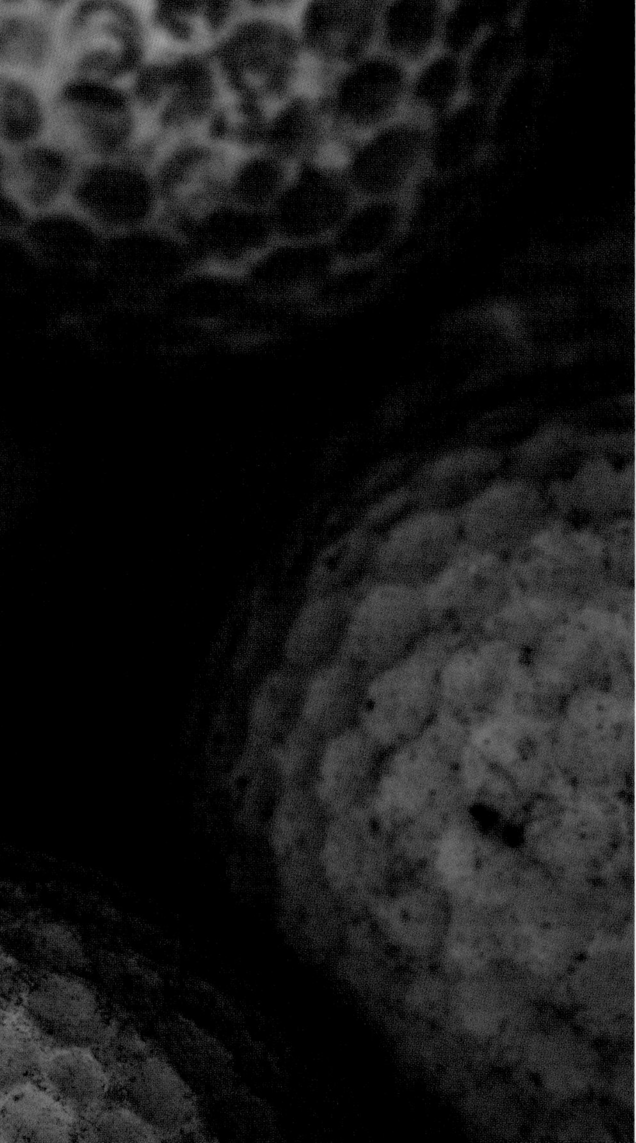

misfortune into moments of genuine pride.

The saying goes that there's no such thing as a bad round of golf because you're still playing golf. Solo golfers understand this on a deeper level: When you have the course all to yourself, there's really no such thing as a bad course. Every round becomes a story, every hole an adventure, and every challenge a reminder of why you love the game in the first place.

Solo rounds are where scuffed balls find renewed purpose.

A SOLO GOLF STARTER KIT

Sure, you might be able to find a popular 18-hole course that will let you tee off first thing or is otherwise (and improbably) open to solo golfers. But in general, you'll have to work a little to find courses where you can play solo easily. Here are some good places to start looking.

THE VENUE	THE VIEWPOINT
NINE-HOLE COURSE	Although often overlooked by serious golfers, nine-hole courses can sometimes be crowded, given the appeal of a "full half round" for people new to the sport, pressed for time, or stamina-challenged. But the flip side is that in areas with lots of 18-hole options, nine-holers can go wanting. So it's a smart idea to research all the nine-hole courses near your home (or destination) and start calling pro shops.
EXECUTIVE COURSE	Like nine-hole courses, these fun tracks—so called because their dramatically reduced distances were thought to be the ideal midday solution for busy management types—sometimes struggle for business. Which is the dream scenario for solo golfers. The shorter holes and lower intensity make them less appealing to competitive golfers but perfect for a quick solo round.
RURAL COURSE	This is a pure probability play. While there are generally fewer options in sparsely populated areas, there's also a better chance that certain days of the week or times of day will make room for a solo golfer. Rural courses often have a slower pace of play and a more relaxed atmosphere, making them ideal for solo rounds. You might even discover a hidden gem with unique features that differ from more crowded urban tracks.

THE VENUE	THE VIEWPOINT
NEW COURSE	On the one hand, these tracks can be much in demand when they open. On the other hand, it may be quite a different story within a few months, especially if the price is high or the golf is too challenging or too easy. But a new course still finding its audience can be a hidden gem for solo golfers, especially during non-peak hours when its novelty hasn't attracted a full crowd. Keep an eye out for courses in the early stages of establishing themselves in the local market.
COURSE IN DISREPAIR	Reddit, the GolfNow app, or some other wisdom-of-the-crowd source can clue you in quickly to poorly maintained courses that have alienated the locals. But what is a turnoff to group golfers is an opportunity for the solo player. These courses often offer lower green fees and fewer players on the course, creating an ideal environment for relaxed experimentation. Just be prepared to navigate some less-than-pristine conditions—think of it as an additional challenge!
STRUGGLING/ CLOSED COURSE	See above. There's almost always a course closing down or nearing that decision within 100 miles of wherever you happen to be. Such links can be lax about all sorts of things, including golfers who—gasp!—turn up to play holes 4 through 12 for a "quick nine." These courses can be gold mines for solo players willing to explore unconventional options. You might not get a traditional round, but you'll have the freedom to roam and create your own unique experience.

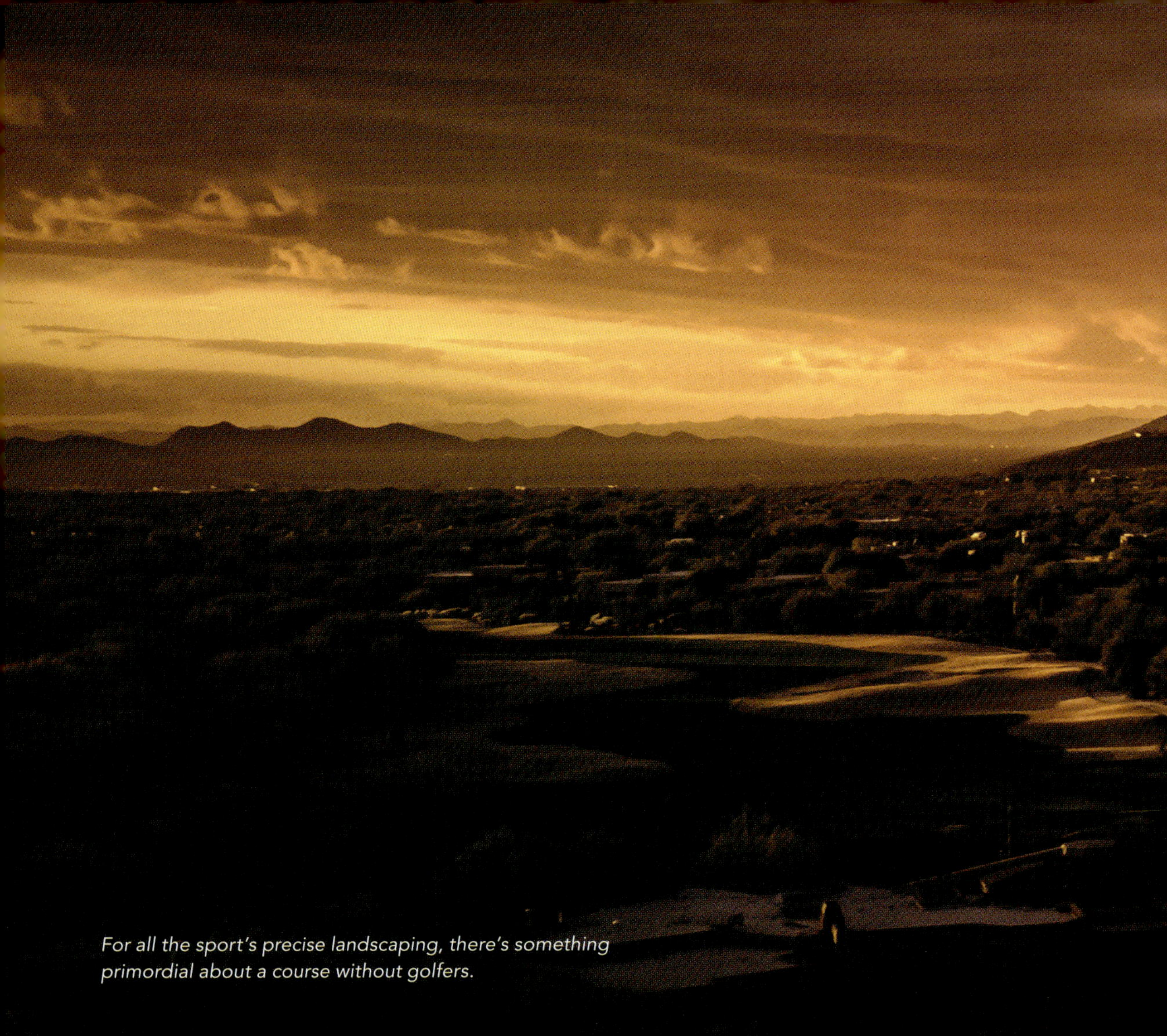

For all the sport's precise landscaping, there's something primordial about a course without golfers.

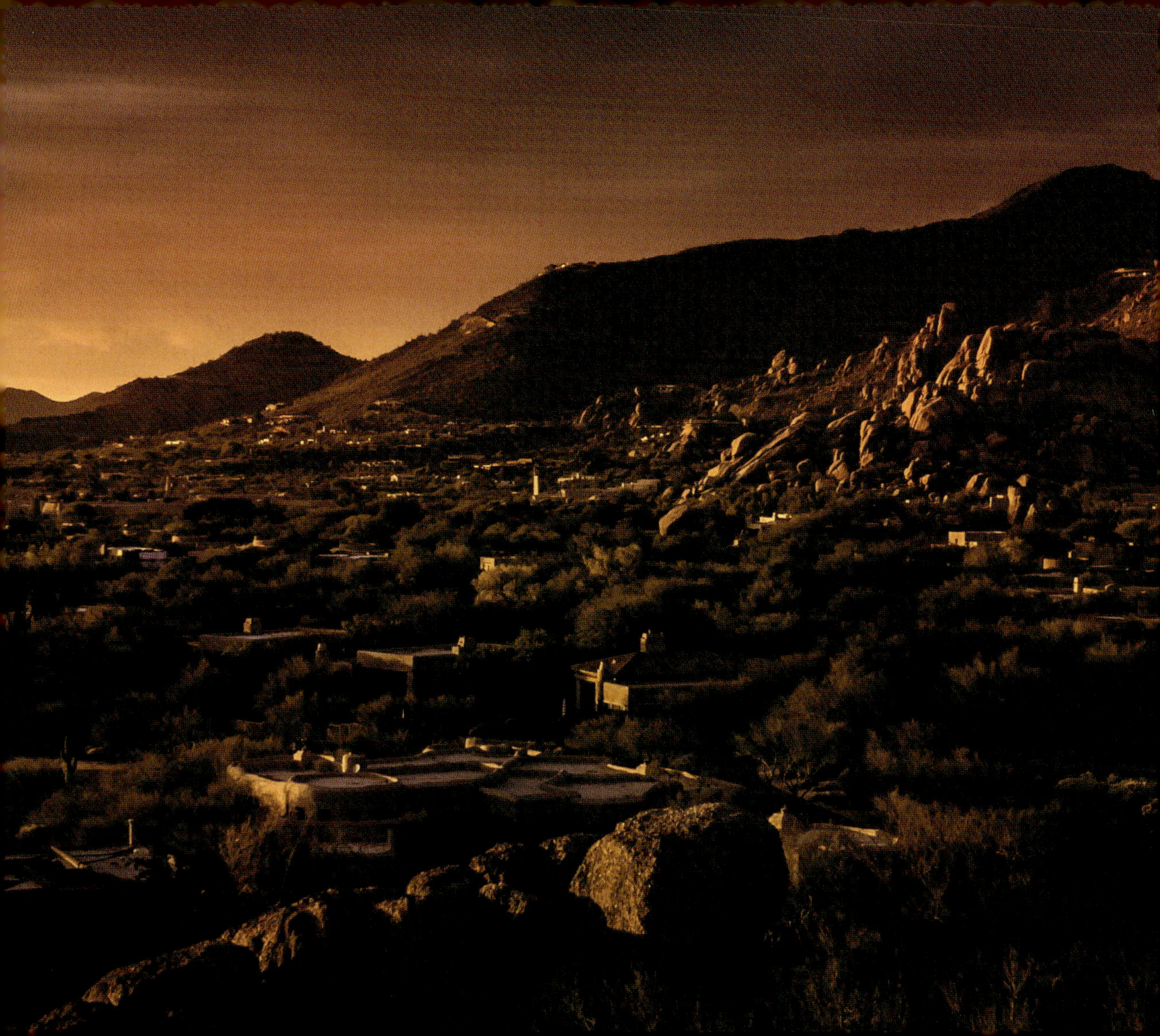

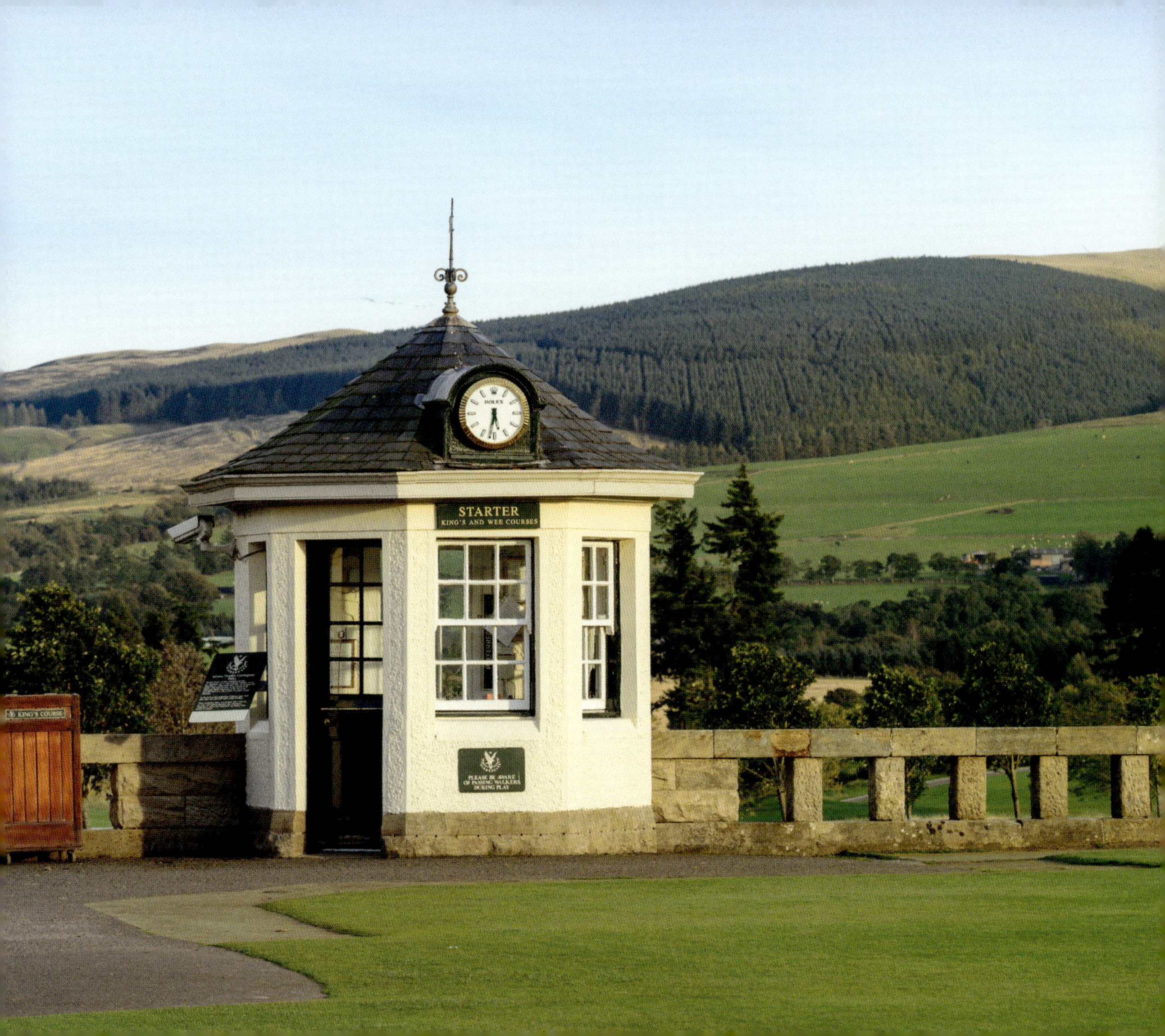
STARTER
KING'S AND WEE COURSES
KING'S COURSE

"The most important thing when you're trying to play alone is the attitude you bring when you ask."

—PIA NILSSON, *LPGA Professional*

How to Book a Solo Tee Time

It's somewhat ironic that setting up a time to play golf alone almost invariably involves other humans. It's exceedingly rare, if not impossible, to secure a solo tee time online with whatever app or platform you favor. (Booking a "single" via the internet—barring rare good fortune—puts you on the first tee box with one, two, or three other golfers.)

Which is to say that as a rule, you have to talk your way into a solo links experience.

And when you do, here are some things to keep in mind. (Note: This advice assumes you're not a member of a club. Because if you are, there's usually a protocol for arranging tee times of any kind, and you should follow it.)

THINK AHEAD. Sure, there's always a story about someone who simply dropped by a local track and knocked off a quick 18 in blissful solitude. But it's a fair bet that most of those stories happened in Scottsdale on a 102°F July afternoon. Which is to say, these stories are rare for a reason: Most solo rounds require planning. Research your local courses and identify which ones are more likely to accommodate singles, such as those with less foot traffic or flexible policies.

REGULARS GET PRIVILEGES. You're more likely to get some love if you're a familiar—and friendly—face. Make an effort to frequent a specific course or two. Building rapport with staff not only increases your chances of securing a solo round but also makes the process feel more personal and enjoyable.

IN-PERSON BEATS OVER-THE-PHONE. In most situations you're asking a course employee to bend or break a rule. So unless you already have a relationship with the person doing the bending or breaking, the more personal the approach, the better. A face-to-face request can convey your sincerity and appreciation more effectively than a call.

START WITH THE STARTER. All things being equal, this conversation will be more private than one with the person behind the pro shop counter. Obviously, wait to make your approach until the starter isn't busy.

. . . unless you're told not to. It is helpful to first ask other course personnel—caddies, maintenance workers, clubhouse attendants, bartenders, food servers—if they know people who have golfed alone, and if so, how they went about it. Maybe they shrug, or maybe they reveal the secret to securing a solo tee time, which might very well be someone other than the starter, e.g., a pro shop staffer or someone else involved in scheduling or booking. You might find that there's an unspoken protocol or even a particular staff member who's more willing to accommodate solo golfers.

. . . or unless you can't. If a starter is inaccessible, someone at the pro shop, either a rank-and-file employee or the manager, is the next best thing. Some pro shop managers appreciate being sought out for such requests and return such deference with an eagerness to please. Be polite but persistent: Many solo golfers have found success simply by showing genuine enthusiasm for the game.

BE STRAIGHTFORWARD, RESPECTFUL, AND UNASSUMING. You are, after all, asking for an accommodation, an exception to the way most courses operate. You might even be entering into a dynamic that puts the person with the power in peril. So be a human.

Your initial salvo can be something as simple as "Hi, I'm trying to figure out if I can play 18 on my own, just me alone, nobody else in my 'group.' Is that something that's ever done here?"

DON'T FLASH CASH. On the one hand, it's perfectly okay—and maybe even expected—to "tip" a starter or pro shop worker or clubhouse attendant after they help you secure a solo tee time. On the other, a blatant attempt to bribe your way onto a tee box could well ruin your chances.

There's no standard way to do this, but an ambiguous statement generally won't hurt. So, after your initial salvo, you might add something along the lines of "I'm happy to pay extra, of course. This is something I really enjoy, so it's worth it to me to pay a little more."

The advantage of this approach is that your intentions remain plausibly fuzzy. Maybe you're offering to tip the course employee, or maybe you're offering to pay some imagined "solo golf fee" (which isn't a thing, as far as I know). Everybody gets to keep their dignity. In my experience, nearly every person who has helped me play solo has made it clear that no tip is required—and each of them has gladly accepted the one I offered.

BE GENEROUS BUT REASONABLE. A good rule is 10 percent of the cost of the round, minimum $10, in part because no one is donating a kidney and in part because it's in the interest of everyone who enjoys playing golf alone to keep costs down. Generosity is appreciated, but overtipping can set unrealistic expectations for other solo golfers trying to secure a tee time. Balance gratitude with practicality.

USE THE DIFFICULTY.

Sometimes, a rejection can lead you to discover a hidden gem, i.e., an out-of-the-way course or a lesser-known spot that welcomes solo golfers with open arms. So if a course simply will not accommodate you, be sure to ask those crushing your dreams for suggestions of courses that might. More often than not, nobody knows more about what's happening at the corner grocery store than the grocer across the street.

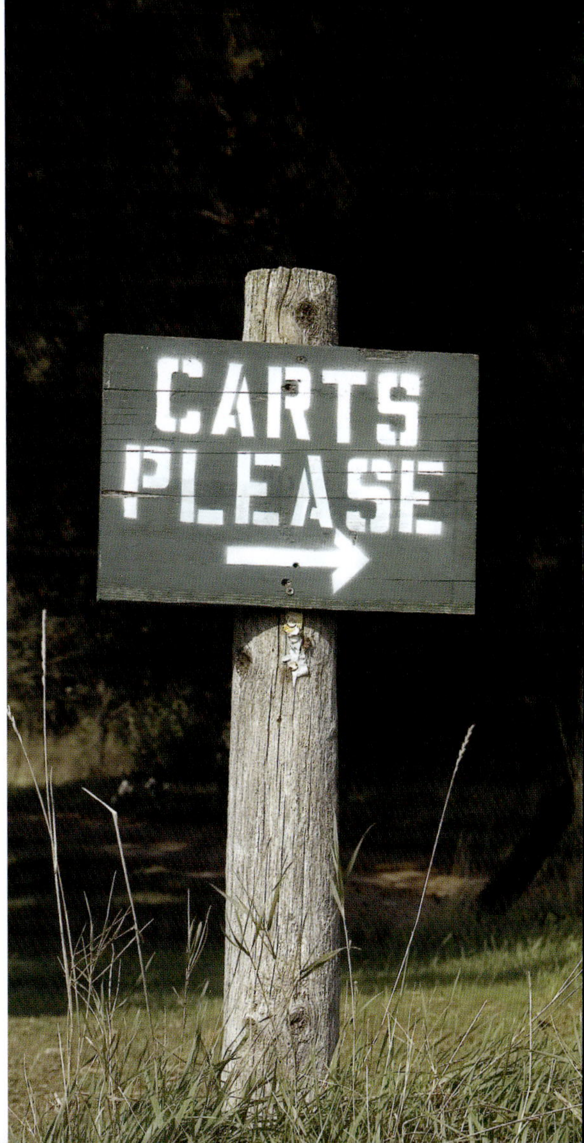

6 GOLF BOOKS TO GET YOU IN THE MOOD

Golf Dreams
by John Updike

Meditations on the games and its subtleties from a Pulitzer Prize–winning writer.

Golf in the Kingdom
by Michael Murphy

If you doubt the spiritual aspects of golf, you won't after reading this classic.

Uneven Lies
by Pete McDaniel

A tour de force take on the Black American experience in golf.

Harvey Penick's Little Red Book
by Harvey Penick

Question: What's the most revered golf instruction manual? Answer: You mean aside from the *Little Red Book*?

The Bogey Man
by George Plimpton

A month on the PGA Tour.

Golf My Way
by Jack Nicklaus

Because—with all due respect to Bobby Jones, Ben Hogan, Arnold Palmer, and Tiger Woods—his way remains the best.

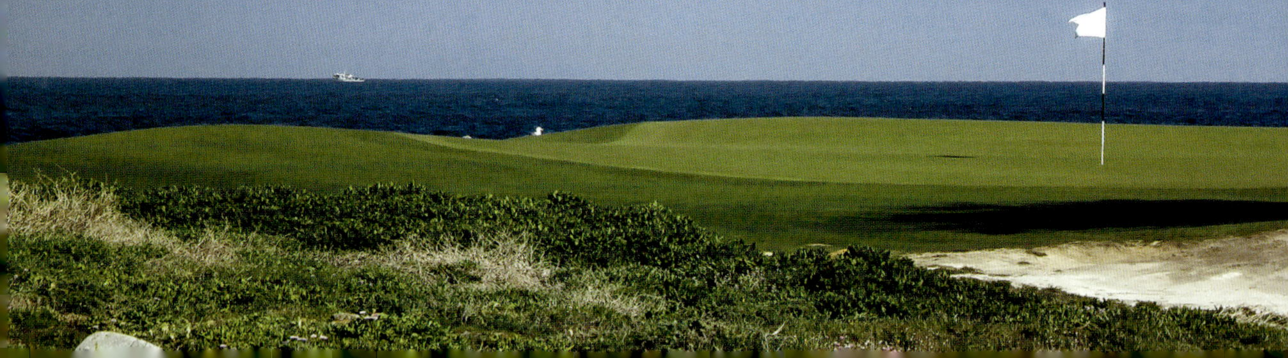

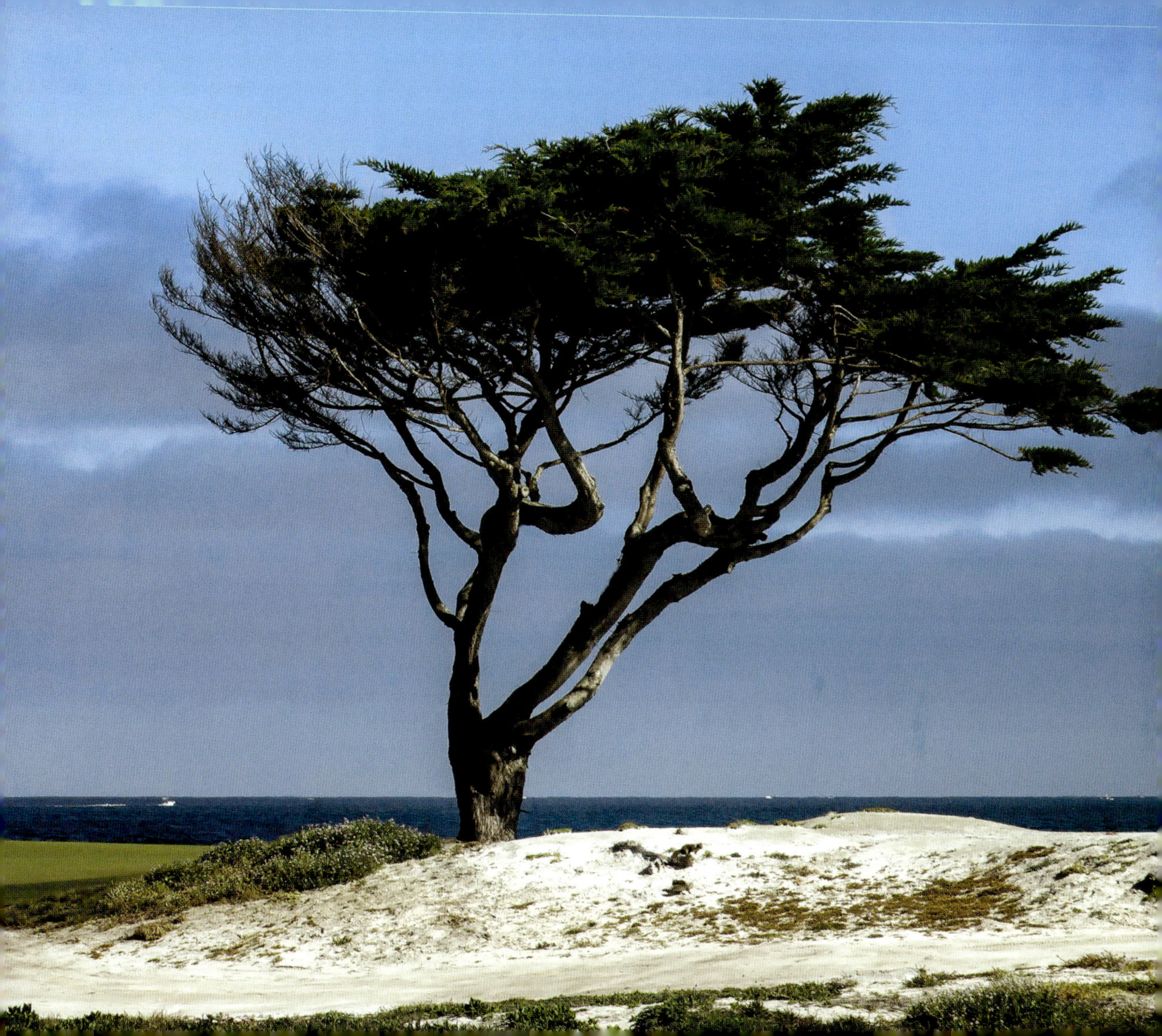

"Singles, for the most part, don't really have a lot of rights on the golf course. Playing alone is an art form."

—BILL FEDDER, *PGA Professional*

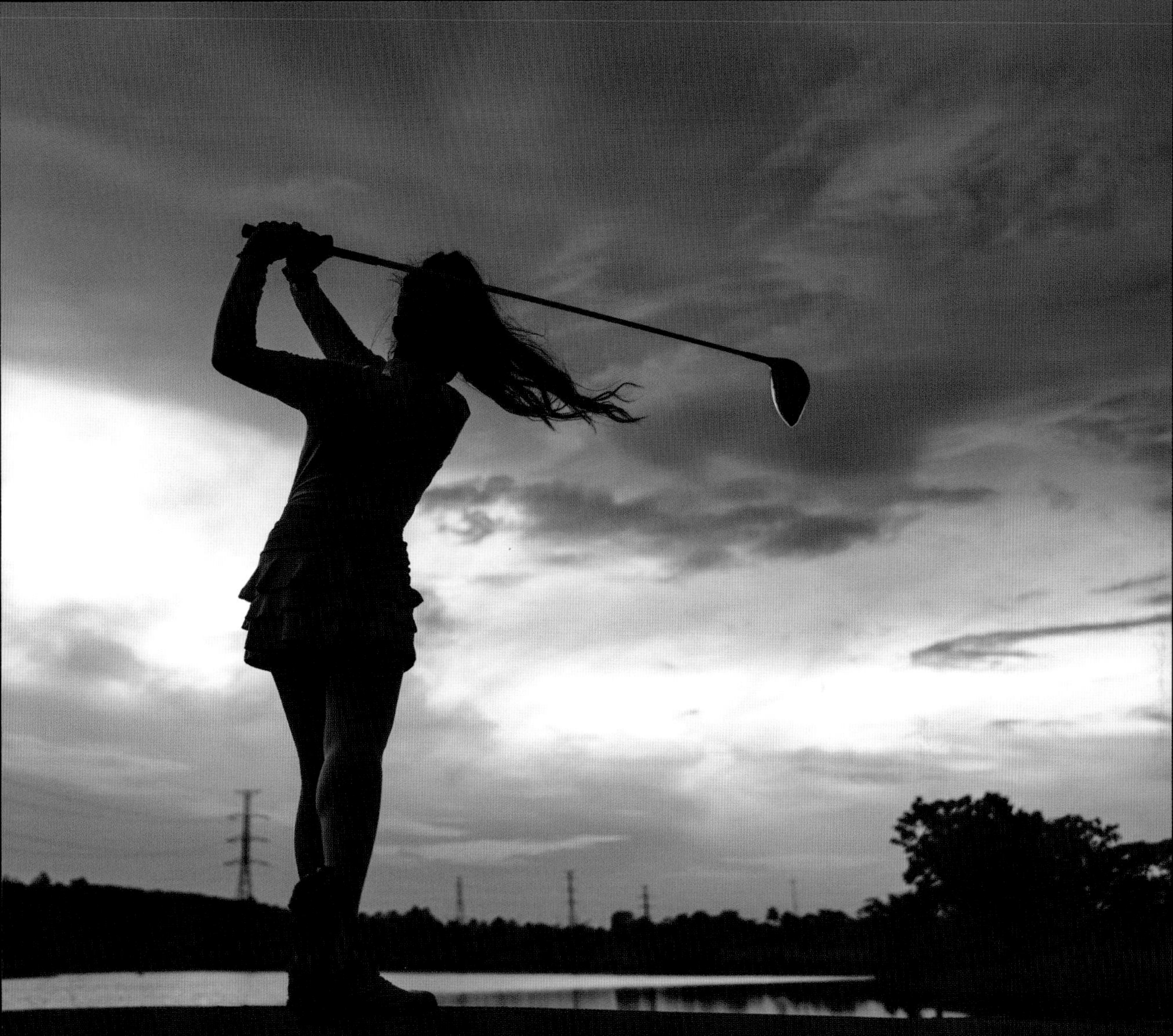

Solo Golf Etiquette

Unless you're fortunate enough to be first off the tee on a given day, a round (or a few holes) of solo golf almost assuredly means you'll have to deal with other humans at some point on the course—and they almost always come in packs.

Such encounters pose two sets of distinct challenges.

The first is practical: how to navigate a course playing at a faster pace than everyone else.

The second is metaphysical: how to maintain a solo golf state of mind—peaceful, focused, contemplative—while attending to the first challenge. Because, to paraphrase (likely non-golfer) Jean-Paul Sartre, when it comes to solo golf, hell is other hackers.

Here, then, are some forged-by-experience rules to help you avoid or overcome the inevitable sticky situation.

BE HUMBLE. On most courses on most days, a solo golfer will have to ask at least one group—but more likely many—for permission to play through. That's okay; every golfer with even a little experience knows this can happen. Which doesn't mean every golfer will be equally accommodating. But remember that you are the exception, not the rule. Playing solo is a privilege, not a right, so operate from a base of humility.

BE AWARE THAT YOU ARE AT THE MERCY OF THE GROUP AHEAD OF YOU. Keep in mind also that playing through one group is fine, but playing through multiple groups in obvious succession—e.g., a par-4 followed by a par-3—is frowned upon. So don't ask to play through if you know that moving ahead will just put you right behind another foursome. Be prepared to wait. Better still, consider skipping a couple of holes. And, as is the case in "normal golf," never ask to play through after the 17th tee. Take a breath and reconsider your club choice.

BE GENEROUS WITH INFORMATION—TO A POINT. Transparency helps establish goodwill. So, when you catch up to a foursome and want to play through, let them know what you're up to. When they're inevitably curious about how you swung a solo tee time, answer *most* of their questions honestly. I say "most" because if you slipped the starter or pro shop guy a tip to facilitate your solo play, you should in all cases keep that to yourself. Some details should remain private, in large part to protect your solo tee time "dealer."

DON'T JUST THINK OF OTHERS; ACT LIKE YOU'RE THINKING OF OTHERS. Once you've been allowed through, do what you can to return the favor. Specifically, don't take longer than you might reasonably be expected to. That means, for instance, limiting range-finder use. And if you begin to struggle, pick up your ball or materially improve your lie. Being mindful of others' time shows respect for the privilege you've been granted. A wave of thanks as you move ahead can go a long way toward leaving a positive impression.

NEVER HIT MULTIPLE BALLS FROM THE SAME POSITION IF OTHERS ARE WAITING. Even if you're certain that you're playing at a faster pace than any group would, you'll annoy those behind you, and some of them might just complain to a ranger or other course employee.

BE FLEXIBLE. If you find yourself having to wait for a group in front of you but have no traffic behind you, consider replaying the hole you've just finished. This can be an opportunity to experiment with different shots or test your skills in various lies. Maybe turn it into a par-3 by walking back to an appropriate approach-shot distance. Sure, go ahead and tee up your ball. In time you'll find that such ad hoc inventiveness adds to the delight of solo golf.

KNOW YOUR PLACE. If you're first off the tee in the morning, you may actually catch the maintenance crew prepping the course. Always defer to their needs. Be vocal (or obviously visual) about your willingness to wait for them to finish. This is especially important if you intend to be a repeat solo customer, but even if you're unlikely to ever play the course again, it's part of the solo golf mindset to remember that you're a little lucky to be there, no matter how much you're spending on green fees (and tips). Their work ensures the quality of the course, and showing them courtesy reflects well on you as a solo golfer.

PLAY TO A CROWD OF YOU. Every golfer, but especially the higher-handicap player, is to some extent conscious of the "audience" watching them play. That awareness of prying eyes is only amplified while playing solo. Reframe this perception by choosing to see yourself as a model of composure, grace, and enjoyment.

INSTEAD OF FOCUSING ON HOW YOU'RE BEING PERCEIVED, FOCUS ON HOW YOU'D LIKE TO REPRESENT THE JOY OF THE GAME. With every action you take, in matters of technique or etiquette, do it right, to your measure of excellence. No frustrated swings after a poor shot, no shouted expletives, no jamming clubs into your bag. Rather, aim to embody the picture of composure and competence.

THE REWARD FOR THIS MINDSET IS NOT JUST HOW OTHERS PERCEIVE YOU BUT HOW YOU PERCEIVE YOURSELF. Confidence comes from understanding who you are as a golfer and fully embracing the joy of the solo experience. When you approach each round with this attitude, you'll find that every hole feels like exactly where you're meant to be.

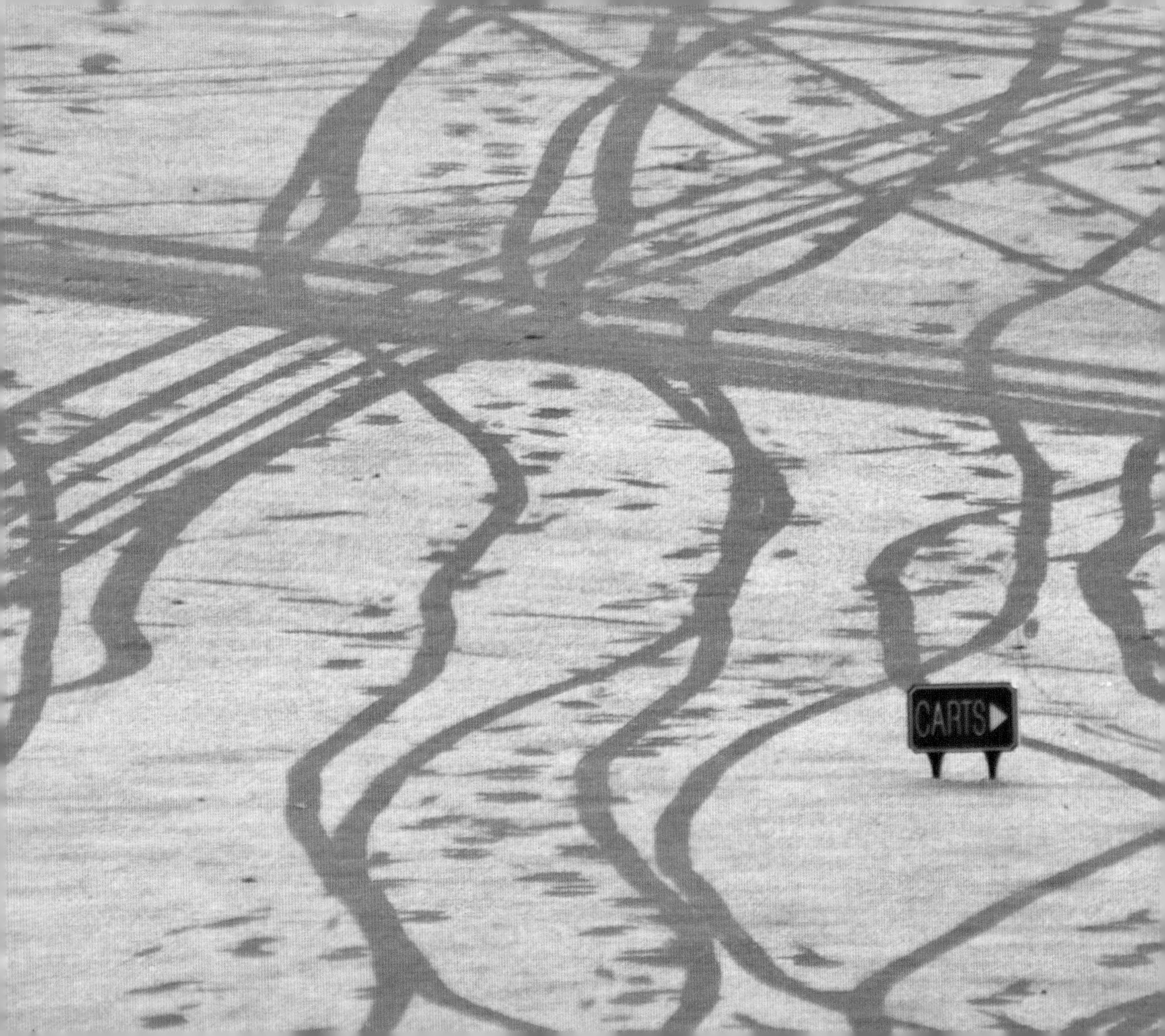
CARTS

"I've played many rounds solo, just for the joy of playing, of experiencing nature in this beautiful park."

—CRAIG GUNN, *PGA Professional*

CONCLUSION

Solo Golf Nirvana on the UNM Championship Course

Here's a true golf story: In 1996, a pair of New Mexico newlyweds unwittingly made their prenuptial agreement a matter of public record when they (needlessly) filed it with the county clerk of Bernalillo County. After news of their exceedingly detailed and exceptionally unusual agreement broke, journalists from around the country besieged the county clerk's office to request copies of the 16-page, single-spaced prenup document, which contained scores of ground rules for the marriage. These various and sundry directives included provisions that nothing ever be left on the floor of their home overnight (except when packing for a trip), that the fuel gauge of their car never drop below half a tank, and that they have "healthy" sex three to five times per week.

It was that last item, more than any of the others, that landed Rex and Teresa LeGalley on *Good Morning America*, one of the hundreds of media outlets that covered the two lovebirds over the ensuing weeks and months. They were in part an early example of internet-fueled celebrity and a late example of traditional media notoriety. (They were also long married: The LeGalley union endured for more than two decades, until Rex's death in 2017.)

I know all of this because, well, I was one of the journalists who sought to understand their marriage. I spent nearly a week with Rex and Teresa in Albuquerque and later wrote a long feature story about them for one of the country's largest-circulation magazines.

But if I'm being honest, I mostly remember that long-ago trip so well for another reason entirely. One afternoon, while husband and wife were at work, I played a round on the Championship Golf Course at the University of New Mexico. There, for the first time in my life, I broke 90.

Needless to say, because I am concluding this book with the story, I was playing solo. And if the very first time I played by myself, in the Pacific Northwest, put me in some kind of Zen trance, this outing in the American Southwest definitely had me in the kind of deep flow state that I described in the very first pages.

For me, on that day in ABQ, all was golf. Off the tee, from the fairway, around the green, on the carpet—it didn't matter where I was or what club was in my hand, I was . . . a golfer.

It's not that my round was without error—or that for one round I somehow conjured the club speed and power that my swing has consistently lacked. Rather, it was as if the chilly conditions, dry air, and, most of all, the beautiful solitude had wrung all the variability and noise from my game.

I was all consistency and signal.

What I intended to do on every shot I pretty much succeeded in doing, all the while building confidence in my ability even as I stopped thinking so much about any of it.

More than any particular shot, I remember the feeling of playing to a metronome; my seven-mile walk of rhythm and breath and vision felt almost otherworldly. I also remember deciding not to add up my hole scores after the front nine. I was happy to be playing well but also vaguely aware that I didn't care about my score as much as I normally would when playing with others.

I did, however, believe that something special was happening. There was a reason I skipped the refreshment options at the turn and floated directly to the 10th tee, where I opted for a 5-iron simply because it just felt right.

And so it went for the rest of the round, the odd shank or sweet swing popping up amid a few dozen perfectly okay golf shots, all doing more or less what they were meant to.

When I totaled all of them up just off the 18th green, I was pleasantly surprised to find that I had shot the best round of my life. And, yes, of course, I knew that although my score was solid, especially for me, it would be nothing to brag about for many other golfers.

Then again, there was nobody else to brag to.

It was just me, alone with my game.

In solo golf heaven.

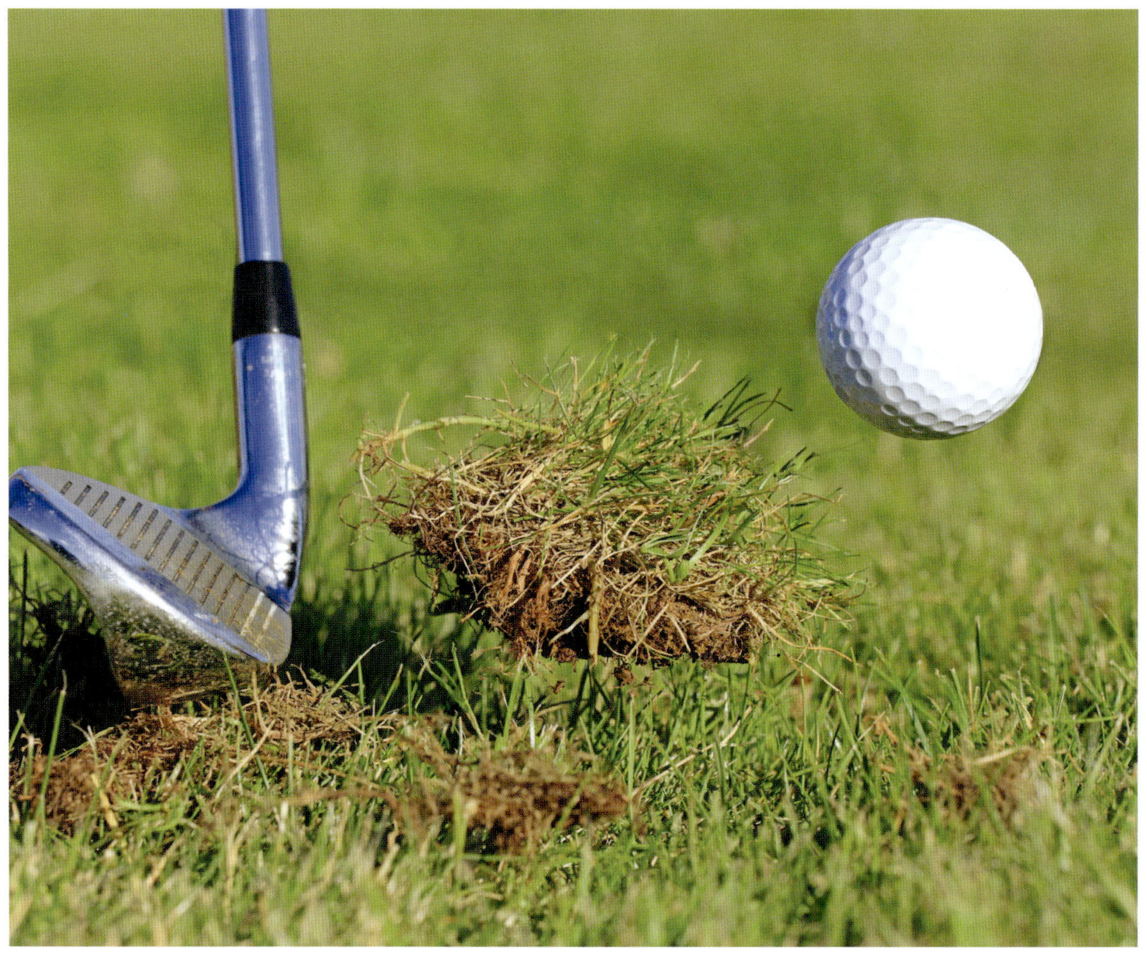

Acknowledgments

Basha Fredman, Tova Rubin, and Lauren Winkleblack, valuable contributors at Elland Road Partners, undertook some early and important research into solo golf.

Anna Katherine Clemmons Clay, journalism professor and journalist extraordinaire, was enterprising, thorough, and insightful in her reporting for this book, not to mention the usual pleasure to work with. In other words, par for the course.

Neil Fine, my business partner at Elland Road Partners, offered front nine guidance and back nine polishing that made a world of difference to the final product.

Lia Ronnen at Hachette has long supported my varied and peculiar sports-related interests, and her colleague Danny Cooper at Workman proved an extremely sharp editor and very helpful sounding board.

And, finally, it was Tyler Mathisen, then an executive editor at *Money Magazine*, who long ago suggested that I bring my clubs on a reporting trip to the Pacific Northwest in case a window of golfing opportunity opened while I was on the road. I will be forever grateful to him for that bit of advice, along with many other professional kindnesses large and small.

Photography and Art Credits

COVER:

Sinica Kover/Shutterstock

INTERIOR:

Alamy: Action Plus Sports Images pp. 22-23; ARphotography p. 142; AZP Worldwide p. 44; Brian Branch Price/ZUMA Wire/Alamy Live News p. 116; Cavan Images p. 5; Kevin Dietsch/UPI p. 65; Tyler Olson p. 79; Rustycanuck p. 147. Shutterstock: BCFC pp. 126-127; BGStock72 p. 98-99; Blapninyo p. 93; bleung pp. 66-67; Francois Boizot pp. 108-109; Neil Bradfield pp. vi-vii; Bonita R. Cheshier p. 41; Dean Clarke p. 148; Connect Images – Legacy p. 105; cornfield p. 128; Sheila Croft pp. 58-59; Daniel50 pp. 70-71; Benoit Daoust p. 110; Alexander Davidovich p. 9 Melanie Decker pp. 18-19; Orest Drozda p. 39; ESB Basic p. 133; Anze Furlan p. 61; Matt Gibson p. viii; Ryan Greene pp. 76-77; Erman Gunes pp. 84-85; Adrian Hughes p. 57; Miks Mihails Ignats p. 152; Isogood_patrick pp. 90-91; LarsZpp. 114-115; Jacob Lund p. 51;melhijad p. 89; MISTER DIN p. 137; moonmovie pp. 46-47; mr.kriangsak kitisak p. 122; Tim Murphy pp. 96-97; NH p. 14 Brandon Olafsson p. 119; Peakstock p. 25; Photoongraphy pp. 68-69; PJ photography p. 72; Brett M Price p. 82; Rich T Photo p. 55; sattahipbeach p. 34; SH Golf Photography pp. 48-49, pp. 106-107; shulers p. 87, pp. 106-107; David P. Smith pp. iv-v; taka1022 p. 33; Ted Pagel p. 29; thetahoeguy pp. 134-135.

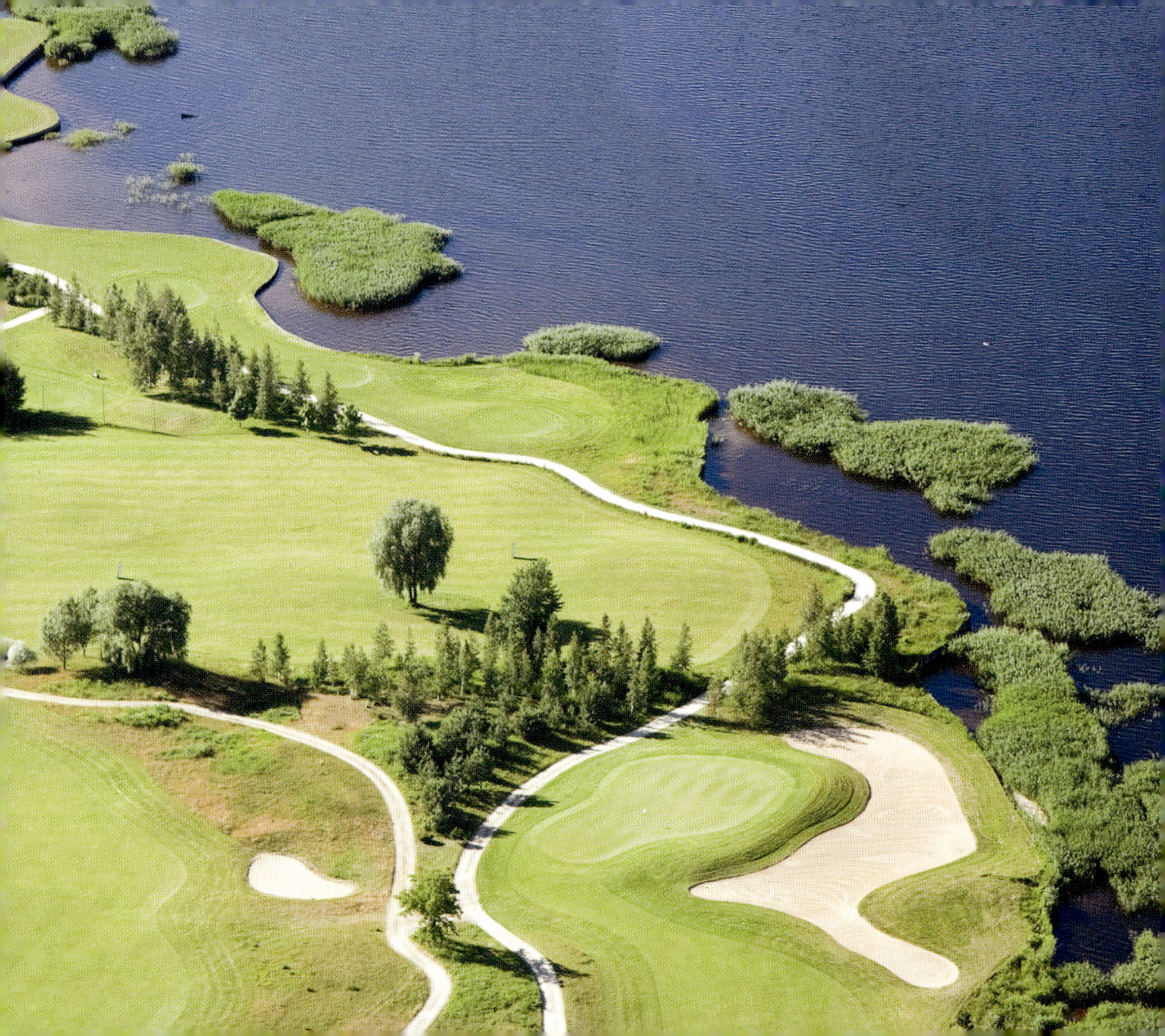